AVID

READER

PRESS

WHERE THE MONEY IS

Value Investing in the Digital Age

ADAM SEESSEL

Avid Reader Press

NEW YORK   LONDON   TORONTO
SYDNEY   NEW DELHI

A<small>VID</small> R<small>EADER</small> P<small>RESS</small>
An Imprint of Simon & Schuster, Inc.
1230 Avenue of the Americas
New York, NY 10020

First Avid Reader Press hardcover edition May 2022

AVID READER PRESS and colophon are trademarks
of Simon & Schuster, Inc.

For information about special discounts for bulk purchases,
please contact Simon & Schuster Special Sales at 1-866-506-1949
or business@simonandschuster.com.

The Simon & Schuster Speakers Bureau can bring authors to your
live event. For more information or to book an event, contact
the Simon & Schuster Speakers Bureau at 1-866-248-3049
or visit our website at www.simonspeakers.com.

Interior design by Paul Dippolito

Manufactured in the United States of America

1   3   5   7   9   10   8   6   4   2

Library of Congress Cataloging-in-Publication Data has been applied for.

ISBN 978-1-9821-8514-5
ISBN 978-1-9821-8516-9 (ebook)

To my parents,
Tom and Diane,
Who taught me to love good writing
And appreciate rigorous inquiry

As a newcomer—uninfluenced by the distorting traditions of the old regime—I could respond readily to the new forces that were beginning to enter the financial scene. I learned to distinguish between what was important and unimportant, dependable and undependable, even what was honest and dishonest, with a clearer eye and better judgment than many of my seniors, whose intelligence had been corrupted by their experience.

—Ben Graham, *The Memoirs of the Dean of Wall Street*

The key to investing is not assessing how much an industry is going to affect society, or how much it will grow, but rather determining the competitive advantage of any given company and, above all, the durability of that advantage.

—Warren Buffett, *Fortune*, 1999

Disclaimers

Certain pricing data and information referenced herein has been provided by ICE Data. ICE Data cannot guarantee the accuracy or completeness of such data and information and accepts no liability in connection with its use.

Nothing in this document should be construed as investment advice or a recommendation to buy or sell any investment products or to make any type of investment. This book shall not constitute an offer to sell or the solicitation of any offer to buy any securities, which may only be made at the time a qualified offeree receives a confidential private offering memorandum or other authorized documentation describing the offering. Information relating to any fund as set forth herein is subject to change.

Any and all information provided herein may be modified or supplemented in subsequent editions of this book.

The investment themes reflected within this book are included merely to illustrate the types of investments that the author may make on behalf of the funds or clients he manages. There is no guarantee that any fund or client will or will not invest in such securities in the future. It should not be assumed that any investment theme or idea discussed herein has been or will be profitable, or that recommendations made in the future will be profitable or will equal the investment performance of the investment themes or ideas discussed herein.

Any performance information, projections, market forecasts, and estimates in this book are forward looking statements and are based upon certain assumptions. Any projections, forecasts, and assump-

Contents

A Note on Terminology

This book contains a fair number of business, financial, and accounting terms. It's a book about investing, after all. However, readers unfamiliar with them should not feel intimidated. Like most engaged in well-paid professions, money managers employ esoteric language to make their job appear more difficult than it is. Such smoke screens, advisors hope, help justify their fees.

As Peter Lynch suggested in his books a generation ago, I believe that investing is too important to be left to the experts. Like Lynch, I also believe that anyone with intelligence, common sense, and their own everyday experience can become a good investor. Indeed, because they are less exposed to short-term pressure, amateurs are often better placed to exploit market opportunities. While the pros fret about their next quarter's performance, amateurs can keep their eyes on the long term, where the real money is made.

That said, accounting is the language of business, and whether you're traveling to a foreign country or the land of commerce, it helps to know the lingo. Here again, don't be afraid. The accounting that investors need to understand is neither mysterious nor terribly complex. At its essence, accounting is just that: it accounts for what a company owns and what it owes, and it helps companies keep track of the money that's coming in and the money that's going out. Accounting is simply a set of rules that businesspeople use to help them keep score, so to speak. As you'll see later in the book, these rules change as economic reality changes. One could argue that, given the rise of the Digital Age, the current system is due for many such alterations.

In the chapters that follow, I do my best to explain in simple terms financial and accounting concepts that might not be intuitive to all. However, if you get stuck, there's a glossary at the end of the book that attempts to define every business and financial term I use. If after consulting the glossary you're still confused, go to Investopedia.com, an excellent, plain-English website that's free to use. If you want to dig even deeper, I recommend a book called *Understanding Wall Street* by Jeffrey B. Little and Lucien Rhodes. It's a short primer that was one of the first books I read when I left journalism and entered finance, and it helped me a lot.

WHERE THE
MONEY IS

Introduction:
So Big, So Fast

I have a friend from college, Alex, whose wealth accumulation strategy over the last fifteen years has been to own a single stock: Apple. Alex bought Apple in 2007, when the company introduced the iPhone, based on the following logic:

A. *I just got an iPhone, and it's such a revolutionary product that a lot more people are going to get one, too—now and for many years to come.*

B. *The stock price is going to follow.*

As the chart below shows, Alex ended up absurdly right. The market average, as measured by the S&P 500 index, is up roughly threefold over this period, while Apple is up roughly forty-five fold.

Apple's wonderful ascent, however, obscures the fact that four times over the last fifteen years, Apple's stock lost 30% of its market value. Once every three to four years, Alex saw his life savings decline by almost a third. As anyone who has ever invested in the stock market can tell you, that does not feel good.

But Alex didn't lose his head, or his lunch, or his conviction in the logic for owning Apple, and he has become wealthy simply by identifying a single, superior business and sticking with it. A $10,000 investment in Apple when the iPhone came out is today worth nearly

Total return since the iPhone was introduced in 2007

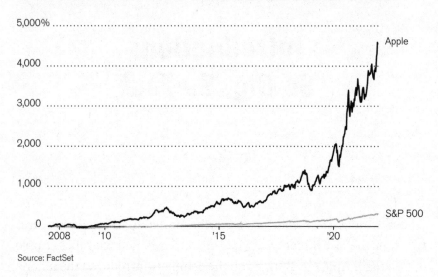

Source: FactSet

$500,000, about fifteen times what he would have made if he'd invested in the S&P 500 index.

Don't get me wrong: the market average represents an excellent return. Despite its wild gyrations and occasional meltdowns, the American stock market has been the best place to build wealth over the last one hundred years. It's no mystery why this is true. Contrary to what many people believe, the market is neither a hall of mirrors nor the Emerald City, where the Wizard of Oz hides behind the curtain pulling the strings. The stock market is nothing more than a collection of American companies whose profits grow over time. As their profits grow, so does their market value. If you believe that the United States will continue to grow and prosper, you should own a piece of that action.

As you'll see below, depending on the index you use and the period you measure, the American stock market has averaged somewhere between 8% and 10% annual appreciation. U.S. real estate, another major way to build long-term wealth, has grown at a materially inferior rate—only 5% a year. In today's interest rate environment, a three-year CD will pay roughly 1% annual interest, while the average commercial checking account pays a pathetic 0.04%.

These numbers sound rather abstract until you grasp the power of compounding. Compounding refers to how something grows—computing power, the profits of a business, the value of a stock—and specifically how growth builds upon itself, gathering momentum and size like a snowball rolling downhill. Because 5% annual appreciation is decent, putting $10,000 to work in the American real estate market over fifty years will net you slightly more than $100,000. But investing that same amount at the average stock market return will generate more than $700,000.

The graphic below illustrates why Albert Einstein called compound interest the eighth wonder of the world. It also shows why you should be invested in the stock market. The younger you are, the more this statement applies, simply because you have more time to allow the market to go through its gyrations and, over time, earn its average return. Even if you're, say, forty years old, I believe you shouldn't have much at all in bonds, which barely pay more than a three-year CD. Some so-called 2045 target date funds have as much as 15% bond exposure in them,

How stocks beat other asset classes

Change in value of a $10,000 investment, by average annual return*

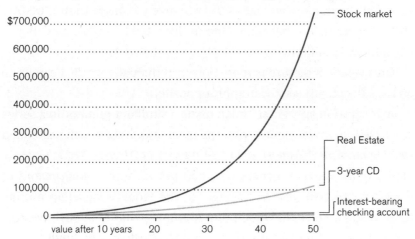

*Based on the following rates of return: Interest-bearing checking account (0.04%); 3-year CD (1%); Real Estate (5%); Stock market (9%)

3

which is 15% too much for me. With more than twenty years ahead of you to smooth out returns, you should be letting the growth of American business work for you.

Investing in the stock market can take either a general or a specific form. Those unfamiliar or intimidated by "the market" prefer a passive approach; they buy an index fund that merely mirrors the stock market average. Other, slightly more adventuresome investors buy exchange-traded funds, or ETFs, which track individual sectors of the economy that they believe will outperform. As for me, I invest in specific stocks. Like Alex with his Apple, I want to find businesses that are going to do better than the market's average of roughly 9% annual growth. In this book, I am going to suggest that you do the same, and I'm going to give you techniques to do so.

Finding a market-beating idea when millions of others are trying to do the same is a real test. It's like solving a complicated puzzle or going on a treasure hunt, and you shouldn't accept this challenge if you're not serious about it. There are plenty of puzzles you can solve and plenty of treasure hunts you can undertake that don't involve your life savings. However, if you apply yourself to identifying, purchasing, and holding above-average stocks, like Alex you can build real long-term wealth. The magic of compounding will see to that: $10,000 invested at the market average of 9% will give you more than $700,000 after fifty years, but that same amount invested at a 12% rate will give you almost $3 million.

Once again, a picture is more powerful than any words I can write on the subject: just see the graphic opposite.

A generation ago, Peter Lynch made a similar argument in a series of bestselling investment books, the most famous of which was called *One Up on Wall Street: How to Use What You Already Know to Make Money in the Market*. Lynch, who had put together a long record of market-beating success as manager of the Fidelity Magellan mutual fund, made an elegant three-point argument that amateur investors can and should build wealth through individual stock picking:

1. **Use your own everyday experience and common sense to identify above-average businesses.**
2. **Invest in them.**
3. **Sit back and let the magic of compounding do its work.**

"In the end," Lynch wrote in *One Up on Wall Street*, "superior companies will succeed and mediocre companies will fail, and investors in each will be rewarded accordingly."

How superior stocks beat the market

Change in value of a $10,000 investment, by average annual return*

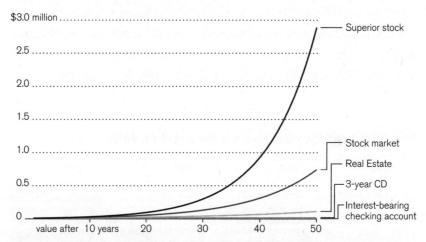

*Based on the following rates of return: Interest-bearing checking account (0.04%); 3-year CD (1%); Real Estate (5%); Stock market (9%); Superior stock (12%)

Lynch's words remain as true as ever, but the problem is that over the last generation technological change has altered the economy so much that the nature and character of what constitutes a superior business has also dramatically changed. The internet, the cell phone, and social media didn't exist when Lynch wrote. Many of the everyday examples that he used to illustrate superior businesses—Toys "R" Us, Subaru, and Hanes, the maker of L'eggs pantyhose—are now laughably out of date. That's no knock on Peter Lynch—the world changes—but we must acknowledge that the same common sense that led him to those stocks now tells us to go nowhere near them. The internal-combustion automobile today faces threats from both driverless and electric cars; most women stopped wearing pantyhose a long time ago; and as for Toys "R" Us, squeezed between the giant pincers of Walmart and e-commerce, it filed for bankruptcy protection in 2017.

Powered by continued improvements in computing power and related technologies, digital companies have transformed our daily lives, the world economy, and—most importantly for purposes of this book—the stock market. Roughly half of the US market's gains since 2011 have come from the information technology and related sectors; since 2016, roughly two-thirds of the market's appreciation has come from these sectors. A decade ago, only two of the world's ten most valuable publicly traded companies not controlled by a government were digital enterprises. Today, as the chart below shows, eight of the top ten are.

World's largest companies by market value

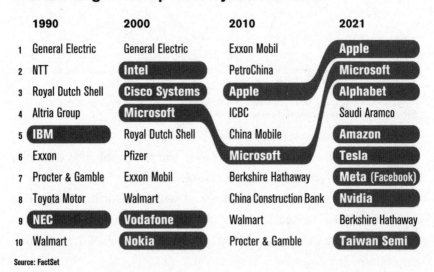

	1990	2000	2010	2021
1	General Electric	General Electric	Exxon Mobil	Apple
2	NTT	Intel	PetroChina	Microsoft
3	Royal Dutch Shell	Cisco Systems	Apple	Alphabet
4	Altria Group	Microsoft	ICBC	Saudi Aramco
5	IBM	Royal Dutch Shell	China Mobile	Amazon
6	Exxon	Pfizer	Microsoft	Tesla
7	Procter & Gamble	Exxon Mobil	Berkshire Hathaway	Meta (Facebook)
8	Toyota Motor	Walmart	China Construction Bank	Nvidia
9	NEC	Vodafone	Walmart	Berkshire Hathaway
10	Walmart	Nokia	Procter & Gamble	Taiwan Semi

Source: FactSet

As the graphic suggests, the Digital Age has come upon us so quickly that we haven't had time to step back and parse what it means. While it's obvious to everyone that something dramatic and lasting has occurred, most investors seem befuddled by it. As a result, most haven't learned the language and the dynamics of a sector whose principal output consists of zeros and ones. To say that this is unfortunate would be an understatement. Companies built on a digital foundation—"tech," in the shorthand of Wall Street—are creating most of the incremental wealth in the world today.

Tech dominates our daily lives so thoroughly that it's natural to think the digital revolution is largely complete, but that's not true. In many ways, it's just beginning. Even after a generation of growth, Amazon's annual retail sales volume only now matches Walmart's. Cloud computing, which today accounts for roughly 10% to 15% of all spending on information technology, will one day likely account for more than two-thirds. Intuit, the world's leading provider of small-business accounting software, reaches only 1% to 2% of its ultimate addressable market. The list goes on, and as computing power compounds, the list gets longer every year.

As tech creates new industries and new wealth, it is simultaneously hollowing out large parts of the legacy economy. Tech's dramatic rise has been accompanied by an astonishing fall in the old economy's market value. Over the last decade, the fossil fuel sector has shrunk from 13% of the U.S. stock market's value to less than 3%. During the same period, the financial services industry has shrunk from 15% of the market to 10%. As recently as 2015, Exxon Mobil and Wells Fargo, two reliable blue-chip investments for generations, were each two to three times more valuable than Amazon. Today, as the chart below shows, Amazon is four times more valuable than Exxon Mobil and Wells Fargo combined.

Big tech gets most of the headlines, but hundreds of smaller, lesser-known tech companies have also continued to appreciate. Adobe in document productivity and digital marketing; Ansys in design-simulation software; and Autodesk in digital construction tools are

Market capitalization, in trillions

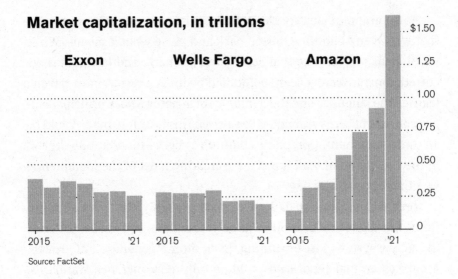

Source: FactSet

only a few examples, and I've not yet exhausted the list of companies beginning with the letter *A*. Most people know Adobe because of its PDF functionality; fewer know that in 2020 Adobe earned roughly $3.5 billion, about the same as Kraft Heinz, whose brands like Oscar Mayer hot dogs and Philadelphia cream cheese have been around since the 1800s.

While the tech revolution began in and remains centered in the United States, its ascent is a global phenomenon. In China, Alibaba and Tencent dominate their digital marketplaces, and SoftBank is one of Japan's ten biggest companies by market capitalization. Germany's most valuable company is database provider SAP, and vibrant start-up cultures exist in nations as varied as India (Flipkart, Reliance Jio), Israel (Wix, Elbit Systems), and Australia (Xero, Altium).

Given all this, if we are serious about building wealth in the Digital Age, we must make a deep and rational inquiry into how we should invest in it. We must understand how tech companies function as businesses, and we must understand the source of their competitive advantage, some of which are old and some of which are new. We also need to learn how to value them, because a tech company's income statement looks quite different from the income statement of an old-economy company. Perhaps most important, we must acknowledge the unspoken central tension facing investors today: confronted with the rise of the digital economy, many of the tools and intellectual constructs that we've relied on for generations no longer work.

Since they began to trade on the open market, companies such as Amazon and Alphabet have looked expensive, and thus unappealing, using traditional metrics. Yet Amazon has appreciated more than 2,300 times since its IPO in 1997, beating the market average by a factor of almost 300. Alphabet is up close to seventyfold since it came public in 2004, beating the market average by a factor of fifteen. Such facts can be explained in only one of two ways: either the market is wrong and we're in for another tech wreck, or many of the traditional yardsticks for measuring value are broken.

Some say that the former is true. Tech's rise, they argue, is nothing more than the second coming of the dot-com bubble, the period in the late 1990s when investors poured money into dozens of tech-related companies as it became clear that online commerce would become a reality. Any enterprise with a "dot-com" at the end of its name rushed to raise money from an enthusiastic public. It was a good party while it lasted—the tech-heavy NASDAQ index quintupled in less than five years—but the hangover was grim. From the bubble's peak in 2000 to its trough eighteen months later, technology stocks lost 80% of their value.

Pessimists are wrong, however, to suggest that we're in for another bust. Today's tech companies have put down powerful and profitable roots in ways that the first wave of dot-com companies never did. Two decades ago, businesses such as Pets.com IPO'd at multi-hundred-million-dollar valuations on the dubious proposition that they were somehow valuable because they attracted lots of "eyeballs." At its peak, however, Pets.com never turned a profit and never generated more than $50 million a year in sales despite spending more than twice that in marketing. Today's online companies don't look anything like Pets.com. Adobe's annual revenues are nearly $16 billion, from which it makes $5 billion in profit. Facebook has 3.5 billion users, and its annual earnings approach $40 billion, which is roughly four times what Disney makes.

Some also believe that, given all the concern over big tech's sudden influence over our lives, government intervention will soon check tech's power and, with it, its ability to generate wealth for shareholders. Governments may well move to curb the influence of the digital giants. They may even succeed in breaking them up altogether—but it's impossible for regulation or legislation to undo a generation of daily, habit-forming usage of the world's largest tech applications. How is any government going to regulate away the fact that, every day, people around the world search on Google 5.5 billion times? Are politicians going to outlaw Facebook from serving its billions of regular monthly users? These companies' applications are woven into the fabric of daily life around the world, and every year the weave gets tighter and stronger. As such, companies like Google and Facebook can rightly be regarded as the Coca-Cola and the General Motors of our generation.

––––––––––

How did tech get so big so fast, and how should we respond as investors? Answering the second question is the subject of this book. Answering the first question provides the context we'll need to answer the second question, so I'll address it here.

The primary reason tech got so big so fast has to do with computing power and the compounding effect of technological change. Computing power has doubled roughly every twenty months since engineers first commercialized silicon transistors in the late 1950s. The cost per unit of computing power was also halved over each of those same twenty-month periods. More power for less money meant that computers and related functionalities like broadband access became exponentially both cheaper and more powerful. When technologists introduced the field-effect transistor, a basic semiconductor that's become the most manufactured artifact in human history, it could hold only a single chip and it cost more than $1. Today, each field-effect transistor contains millions of chips and costs $0.000000001, or one billionth of a dollar.

This price/performance explosion became known as Moore's law, and it's been in force now for more than sixty years. Engineers have been predicting the death of Moore's law for at least a decade, but so far it hasn't happened. Meanwhile, computing's record of delivering more for less has so far been astonishing. From 1959 until 2000, silicon chips became 30 million times more powerful while costing roughly the same. This was a huge advance, but it wasn't powerful enough to drive the massive technological change we see around us today. At the turn of the millennium, only 1% of the world's population had a broadband internet connection, as the venture capitalist Marc Andreessen pointed out in a seminal essay a decade ago. Cell phones were so expensive then that only 15% of the world's population owned one. Such facts help explain why the dot-com boom busted: the technological backbone wasn't strong enough yet to support it.*

In the last decade or so, however, computing power and related functionalities hit a tipping point that enabled the revolution we see today. Today, more than half the world's population has both broadband access and a powerful smartphone. As a result, much of the world searches, shops, chats, banks, and performs many other everyday activities online.

Why do we do so? Because it's better than the old way of doing things! The Olympic motto is *"Citius, Altius, Fortius"*—"Faster, Higher, Stronger." Tech's motto, if it had one, would be *"Citius, Parvius, Melior"*—"Faster, Cheaper, Better." Digital applications save us time, save us money, and make our lives easier and better in multitudes of big and

---

* Anyone interested in this subject would enjoy reading Andreessen's "Why Software Is Eating the World," first published in the *Wall Street Journal* in 2011. Likewise, you should read Gordon Moore's less elegantly titled "Cramming More Components onto Integrated Circuits," a 1965 essay that laid out the price/performance dynamics of computing power. The former is five pages long and the latter is four pages. Why are all the most important papers so short?

little ways. Before Google Search, you had to go to the library or invest in a set of encyclopedias, which were bulky, went quickly out of date, and were hardly interactive. Before digital maps, you needed paper maps, which often ripped, never folded properly, and didn't give you alternate routes or reports on traffic accidents along the way. Before Facebook and Pinterest, groups relied on actual bulletin boards rather than digital ones.

Such improvements are the second reason tech got so big, so fast: tech makes better mousetraps. Rocket Mortgage can secure you a cost-competitive home loan online in half the time that a brick-and-mortar bank can. Intuit offers its small-business customers an everyday cash balance interest rate of 1%, which is twenty-five times higher than the average legacy commercial bank. Amazon recently estimated that it saves an average Prime customer seventy-five hours a year in trips to physical stores. Multiply that by 200 million Prime subscribers, assign a $10-an-hour value to their time, and even after deducting the Prime membership fee you get $125 billion of "time is money" savings. This faster/better/cheaper dynamic holds true for businesses as well. A digital ad on Google or Facebook is not only cheaper than a comparable one on prime-time television, it's also much more targeted and effective, because its impact can be tracked.

Society is now focused on the threats that the big tech platforms pose across a whole spectrum of issues, and rightly so. It's important that we strike the proper balance between privacy and the flow of information, freedom of speech, and undue political influence. As investors, however, we should not forget why people adopted these technologies in the first place. They either improve our lives, reduce our costs, or both. A recent MIT study led by Erik Brynjolfsson quantified how much consumers value their everyday tech applications. He and his team asked consumers how much money it would take to get them to forsake their accounts at Facebook, Google, and others. On average, the study found, it would take $550 in annual payments to make a Facebook user quit Facebook. The number was much higher, nearly ten times so, for WhatsApp. Almost unbelievably, the study found that to go without Google, the average user would require a $17,500 annual payment. That's almost one-third the average American citizen's income.

Couple this utility with what might be called "digital economics" and you have the third and final piece of the puzzle explaining tech's rapid rise in the market. The world has never witnessed such powerful business models. A mature software company operating at scale carries profit margins that are three to four times higher than the average American corporation. Even ambitious tech companies that spend aggressively to grow their business are more profitable than old-economy businesses with high margins. Intuit, the small-business software provider, has profit margins twice that of Campbell's, the soup maker, even though Intuit spends roughly four times as much in marketing, sales, and research and development.

How can that be? Campbell's raw materials are tomatoes and chicken and noodles, which cost a lot; Intuit's raw materials are non-physical and therefore cost almost nothing. Moreover, software-based enterprises like Intuit have no major capital or manufacturing needs. When Campbell's wants to make more soup, it must build a new production line or a new plant. Even Coca-Cola, which sells sugar water, must have its subsidiaries build a bottling plant and invest in trucks and vending machines to expand. Software companies don't require factories or production lines; they require laptops manned by intelligent engineers. When a software company wants to enter a new geographic market, its engineers write new code, hit "deploy," and their software is available around the globe, instantaneously and with almost no incremental costs. Even a software company's major capital requirement, giant servers that process and store data, can now be rented rather than bought. That's the essence of cloud computing.

Higher profitability + lower asset intensity = the highest return on capital businesses ever seen. When Ford wants to grow its business, it must invest $10 in assets to generate $1 in profit. Coke requires roughly $6. Facebook, only $2.

Like most revolutions, the digital revolution has not been orderly. Technology has not only given us ubiquitous consumer applications, it's also given us entirely new asset classes and new ways of trading existing ones. It took human beings millennia to agree on gold as a medium of exchange; bitcoin gained traction in less than a decade. Stock market speculators have always been with us, but they now can place their bets wherever they have cell reception. Recently, they banded together on social media and used new trading platforms to cripple professional short sellers.

Given such turbulence and confusion, an inexperienced investor might reasonably ask: Why should we invest in the stock market at all?

The answer is not complicated. We invest our money because, while it would be nice to spend all of it today, we know that we'll require some down the road. We will need money to put our kids through college, to help our parents get long-term care, and to make sure we ourselves can live comfortably during retirement. We forgo the pleasure of spending $1 in the present to transform that $1 into $5 and then $10 to use at some time in the future. And as I laid out earlier, for the last one hundred years the U.S. stock market has been the best place to do that.

Given the rise of the digital economy, however, we're going to need to modify both our worldview and our toolkit if we're to invest well in the early twenty-first century. Peter Lynch told us to "invest in what you know," and this is generally good advice. Like hunters, investors do best when they understand the terrain. Many older investors, however, today find themselves in an unfamiliar landscape. What do companies with nonsensical names such as Chegg, Splunk, and Pinduoduo do, anyway? And how can we trust the "executives" in hoodies who run them? Mature investors have learned to grow their wealth by investing in old-economy industries like banking, energy, and brick-and-mortar retail, but all these businesses are being co-opted by digital enterprises. As a result, much of what more experienced investors are familiar with is now, from an investment perspective, useless.

Younger and less experienced investors have the opposite problem. They grew up in the digital ecosystem, and they know the territory in that intuitive, born-with-it way that positions them to hunt and track today's investment opportunities. On the other hand, many younger investors mistrust the markets and "the system" in general. They have legitimate reasons. Young investors have already endured three major market meltdowns—the dot-com bust in 2000–2001, the financial crisis in 2008–2009, and the coronavirus pandemic in 2020—and they have entered adulthood with lower incomes and more debt than their parents. No wonder that, rather than turning to reliable investments to build wealth as their elders did, the younger generation has turned to newer, more experimental asset classes like cryptocurrency, socially responsible stocks, and speculations promoted on Reddit message boards.

Don't get me wrong: I dislike crypto as an investment not because it's young and I'm not. I dislike cryptocurrency for the same reason I dislike gold. Neither crypto nor gold are living, dynamic businesses that can expand over time. Bitcoin may be a new storehouse of value, but in the end it's just a currency. It has no customers, no revenues, and no profits to grow.

We thus find ourselves at an odd point in history: older investors understand markets but not technology, while younger investors understand technology but not markets. If either group is to succeed in turning $1 into $5 and then $10 through the force of compounding, this dynamic must change.

In many ways, changing it is remarkably easy. Like Lynch's investment discipline, it can be broken down into three steps:

1. We must remind ourselves that the stock market is nothing more than a collection of businesses and that investing in them has historically been the best way to build wealth.
2. We should acknowledge that the world's economy is increasingly digital, so we must learn how digital companies create wealth.
3. We should invest in the best such companies, then let compounding do its job.

Approached this way, tech's rapid ascent and all its associated dislocations are not reasons to be frightened or disoriented—they're reasons to be excited. It's true that digital companies look nothing like the dominant enterprises of a generation ago, but it's also true that, like all industries, the tech sector follows certain rules. We can study these rules, understand them, and invest accordingly. The world is changing, and we can profit from it.

———————

No subset of investors has had a harder time adapting to the changes brought on by the Digital Age than value investors, an investment discipline of which I'm proud to be part. Although the term is often used, "value investing" is rather hard to define. Just as there are many sects of Christianity, so are there many branches of value investing. Some schools focus on a company's assets, while others concentrate on a company's earnings, and even these subgroups analyze assets and earnings differently. As a result, no value investor practices value investing in the same way, a phenomenon exacerbated by the independent and ornery temperament that most investors possess.

Value investing does, however, revolve around a few central principles. Chief among these is an insistence upon discipline, rigor, and study. Value investors approach the stock market not as a betting parlor or a bodega where we can buy a lottery ticket but as a place where we can systematically attempt to build wealth. We are not traders or speculators. We are bookish and analytical, and we love metrics, yardsticks, and ratios—anything that can help us make sense of the public markets. Above all, we seek to codify our approach to investing through a set of rules. We use a framework that we impose on the stock market so that when we beat it, it's not a matter of luck, but rather of a system.

Value investors are also notorious cheapskates who hate to pay a high price for an investment. That's why we're called "value" investors and that's why we look down on other methods that give price less weight in the decision-making process. We disdain so-called growth investors, who are interested mainly in companies with steep sales and earnings trajectories. We are even more disgusted by momentum investors, who do in fact treat the market like a casino, seeking to ride their luck by following short-term trends.

Because of value investing's disciplined approach, study after academic study has shown that a value-based discipline has led to long-term, market-beating results.* Faced with technology's radically new and alien business models, however, value investing's frameworks have begun to break down. Reliable value-based metrics like price to book value, which measures how expensive a company is relative to its assets, and price to current earnings, which measures expensiveness in relation to how much profit a company is generating, have failed to capture tech's enormous value creation. As a result, these same academic studies are now beginning to show that value investing hasn't been working the way that it once did.†

Even Warren Buffett, the high priest of value investing and widely considered the most successful investor of all time, has struggled to navigate the new economic landscape. While Buffett's long-term returns remain awesome in the original sense of the word, they have been diminishing. As the following chart shows, his market-beating performance peaked in the 1980s, lessened in the 1990s, and since 2017 has turned into underperformance.

How should value investors respond? Do we "just buy the FAANG stocks," as many momentum-based talking heads recommend? Or can we find a new method, a revised discipline that can help us understand what has made tech so big, so fast? Can we devise a system to evaluate and analyze tech stocks so that we can take advantage of the wealth they're creating? Value investing is a flexible and practical construct.

---

* See for example Eugene F. Fama and Kenneth R. French, "Value Versus Growth: The International Evidence," *Journal of Finance* 53, no. 6 (1998): 1975–99, http://www.jstor.org /stable/117458. "Long term" here means a decade or more.

† See for example Baruch Lev and Anup Srivastava, "Explaining the Recent Failure of Value Investing," New York University, Stern School of Business, October 2019, https:// papers.ssrn.com/sol3/papers.cfm?abstract_id=3442539.

Berkshire Hathaway vs. S&P 500

Trailing 10-year performance difference

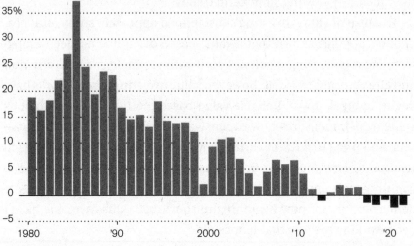

Note: Annualized returns as of Dec. 31, 2021
Source: S&P Dow Jones Indices

It's evolved at least once since it was introduced a century ago. Can it evolve again to encompass the Digital Age?

I believe it can, and this book suggests one such way. As a Wall Street investment analyst since 1995, I've watched as tech stocks have grown from gawky adolescents into some of the most powerful economic specimens the world has ever seen. For the last several years, I've been wrestling with these issues as both a full-time money manager and as a contributor to *Barron's* and *Fortune*. In this book, I do my best to resolve them.

Honestly, I'd rather not have had to investigate "tech" at all. Only a half dozen years ago, I was a stodgy value investor who was comfortable with the old orthodoxies. I'd have been happy to spend the next twenty-five years of my investing career in the same way I'd spent the first twenty-five. I have no innate interest in technology, I dislike gadgets, and I barely understand how electricity works. If it weren't so financially dangerous to do so, I'd stay set in my ways—but old industries are dying and new ones are being born at a rate not seen in more than a century. To continue as I had would have been to ignore economic reality and to consign myself and my clients to a future of dismal performance.

I arrived at this conclusion only after several years of struggle, research, and contemplation. I came to it unwillingly, with the same reluctance that a true believer gives up his faith. But as a student of business, and as someone devoted to what might be grandiosely called Truth, I had to admit that something important had happened. So I recalibrated my instruments and focused my attention on the digital economy. I did this not because tech is sexy, or interesting, or beneficial to society. I did it for the same reason Willie Sutton robbed banks: it's where the money is.

PART I

Preparing to Invest

CHAPTER 1

The World Has Changed

When I began my career in finance twenty-five years ago, I believed, as most people unacquainted with the ways of Wall Street do, that I was entering a testosterone-filled world of sharks and cowboys who spent their days shouting into telephones and gesticulating on the stock exchange floor in a language only they could understand. As this image suggests, my understanding was muddled. I soon came to learn that what really drove markets was a subculture completely unlike the crude images that I and many others held in our imaginations.

My first job was at Sanford C. Bernstein, a firm known for the thoroughness of its investment research, and its halls were as quiet as a monastery's. Bernstein had a team devoted to each of the world's major business sectors—banks, automobiles, pharmaceuticals, and so forth—and the analysts worked behind closed doors. Most reminded me of the professors I'd had in college. Distracted and deep in thought, they would emerge from their offices only to eat or relieve themselves. Kenny Abramowitz, the healthcare analyst, used to walk to the bathroom so fast that his shirttails would come untucked and flap behind him.

The mantras of a good investor, I learned, are the same as those of a monk: study, learn, and practice devotion to your discipline. Good investors do not live by testosterone or adrenaline; they ignore them. Peter Lynch said that his most valuable course in college had nothing to do with finance—it was a course on logic. To relax, Warren Buffett reads the philosopher Bertrand Russell and plays bridge. Buffett guards his thinking time so religiously that, according to his partner, Charlie Munger, his weekly calendar often has only a single activity on it: "Haircut."

Coming as I was from the world of journalism, this kind of measured, monastic rhythm shocked me. Driven by the news cycle, journalism offers plenty of opportunity for crisis and drama—but there are no deadlines in investing. Urgency, I came to learn, induces poor decisions. Good investors show up at their desks every morning with the goal of slowly advancing their understanding. You sit there and study a business; when you finish, you choose from three alternatives: invest, reject, or, most often, wait and watch. Later, as the circumstances change, so does your opinion; meanwhile, you've researched other businesses and formed other conclusions about them. Then the facts surrounding those businesses change, so your conclusions change, and before long you come to resemble neither a cowboy nor a shark so much as a mapper of tides, a riverboat pilot on Mark Twain's Mississippi.

This slow, incremental approach especially characterizes long-term investors, who don't see the stock exchange as a gambling hall in which we "play the market." Instead, we see it as a place where, over time, value is *found out*. One of my early newspaper mentors, a tobacco-chewing investigative reporter named Pat Stith, used to say, "Sooner or later, you get to be known for who you are," and the same is true of stocks. The cowboys may ride the momentum and the sharks may circle a hot stock for a time, but in the end such drama has little bearing on what makes stocks appreciate or not. As Peter Lynch has said, superior businesses win in the stock market over time. Inferior ones either languish or die.

Working in the 1980s and 1990s, Lynch was an intellectual descendant of Ben Graham, Warren Buffett's teacher and the father of modern security analysis. Confronted with the speculative markets of the early twentieth century, Graham imposed an investment discipline onto them. The methods he devised have given generations of investors the chance to approach the market so that positive results stem not from luck, but from a system. Graham's approach came to be known as value investing, and while the discipline has morphed into different schools and subsets, all of them continue to revolve around a few central orthodoxies. All value investors do their research. All value investors are disciplined about the price they pay. Above all, all value investors scorn randomness; instead, like Graham, we impose a framework onto the markets. We invest using a set of rules that we rarely alter, trusting that our discipline will help us outperform the market averages over time.

At Bernstein, our particular framework was called "reversion to the mean," which is a mathematical term for the simple idea that life eventually returns to normal. While economic sectors like energy and financial services go in and out of favor in the stock market, reversion to the mean holds that nothing essential changes in the world's economy. If manufacturing stocks are one day expensive relative to their historical averages, reversion to the mean posits that they will eventually return to a normal, lower valuation. If retail stocks are cheap when measured on historical metrics, they will eventually appreciate.

It's important to note that "expensive" in a stock market context does not mean a high stock price. Stocks aren't measured like gasoline or groceries, where it's axiomatic that a higher dollar value means the goods are more expensive. A business in general, and a stock in specific, is cheap or expensive only relative to something. When judging stocks' expensiveness or cheapness, investors triangulate between their price and some measure of its value. Ben Graham usually measured price against a company's net asset value—its assets less its liabilities—while Buffett focuses more on a company's profit stream.

The reversion to the mean framework measures stocks as Buffett does, comparing a business's current quoted price to its profits, and the essence of the discipline can be summed up by value investor Sir John Templeton's dictum, "The four most dangerous words in the English language are 'this time it's different.'" At Bernstein, this phrase was our Apostle's Creed. Don't try to predict wholesale change, we were taught, because it's not going to happen. Simply buy the companies that are historically cheap and sell the ones that are historically expensive. Eventually, life will return to normal.

I was the junior oil and gas analyst apprenticed to the senior one, and it was our job, along with all the other analysts, to feed data about the companies we covered into what we called "the black box." This wasn't a box at all, but rather a sophisticated computer model Bernstein used to determine statistical cheapness using mean reversion calculations. In would go data on projected sales, estimated earnings, debt ratios, and so forth, and out would come the stocks and the sectors that the black box deemed expensive and the ones it deemed cheap. By selling the former and buying the latter, Bernstein filled its clients' portfolios with well-known American corporations that happened to be on sale. We owned Exxon and BP when energy was out of favor, and we owned Sears and JCPenney when retail was cheap.

Because in the late twentieth century everything did eventually return to normal, the black box generated large gains for the firm and its clients. At its peak, Bernstein managed $800 billion, making us one of the largest money management firms in the world.

The man who presided over the black box when I was there was Lew Sanders, Bernstein's chief investment officer. Lew was slim and quiet, and he moved through Bernstein's corridors with the quiet grace of an abbot in his priory. Lew embodied the kind of cerebral, tide-mapping investor I wanted to be. I used to watch him as he stood for hours absorbing information from one of Bernstein's communal Bloomberg terminals. His eyes were the palest, clearest, and iciest blue I've ever seen, and when he was in front of that computer, they were the only part of his anatomy that moved. They would dart left to right, pausing to focus, then move again across the screen. His fingers would periodically flick across the keyboard to access a new dataset, and his eyes would then resume their progression.

This is how real investors hunt, I remember thinking. They don't move. They stay still and watch.

———————

When I felt my apprenticeship at Bernstein was done, I left to become a more senior analyst at first one and then another firm, Baron Capital and Davis Selected Advisors. In 2000, I began co-managing a mutual fund for Davis, and by 2003 I felt experienced enough as a value investor to start my own firm.

In my new business, I combined techniques like reversion to the mean with some of Ben Graham's original methods, like buying stocks at or below their liquidation value. A decade later, I had built a record of beating the S&P 500 market average after deducting my management fees. I was proud of what I'd done, I'd made money for my clients and myself, and I saw little reason why I'd ever have to change.

Then, in the middle of the last decade, my system rather suddenly stopped working.

I remember sitting at my desk in the late afternoon on New Year's Eve 2014. Unlike Lew Sanders's gaze, mine was unsteady. First I would look at the Empire State Building, which was glowing cheerfully in the winter gloom; then I would look at a printout of my portfolio, which was not. That year, the market had advanced 13% to 14%, but my portfolio had declined 4% to 5%. You don't need to know a lot about investing to recognize that's a huge gap.

All my investments had been made using standard value-investing principles, but none were paying off. I owned shares of Tribune Media, a collection of TV stations and newspapers that could theoretically be liquidated for more than I'd bought the stock. Tribune had recently appointed a young new CEO with a good track record at Fox Broadcasting. Instead of trading upwards to its liquidation value, however, Tribune's shares continued to decline. I owned shares of Avon Products, the door-to-door beauty company, which also had a poor 2014. Two years earlier, a billionaire family specializing in consumer products companies had offered $23 per share to take Avon private. Avon rebuffed them, the stock declined, and I smelled value. My cost was $12 per share, a knowledgeable private buyer had offered $23, but as 2014 ended, the stock sat at $9.

My portfolio was filled with other such companies. FreightCar America, which made rolling stock for railroads, and Seventy Seven Energy, an oil services company, were classic reversion-to-the-mean stocks, bought because they were cheap relative to historical averages. Experience had taught me that they should soon appreciate—but so far the opposite had happened.

Like all value investors, I was accustomed to stocks initially trading below where I bought them. In the short run, as Ben Graham famously said, the stock market is a voting machine—but in the long run it's a weighing machine. It's a place where, over time, the true value of a business gets found out. The essence of value investing is to buy a stock when the market is voting on it, then wait until the market weighs it.

Sitting at my desk that dark December evening, however, I had the uncomfortable feeling that the market had finished weighing my stocks and found them wanting.

The companies I owned shared two characteristics. First, they were all cheap stocks, and historically that had been a good quality. Second, however, all of them likely had their best days behind them. Avon had some growth potential overseas, but door-to-door beauty sales was a declining business in the United States and Europe. Much of the business was moving online. Tribune's newspapers and television stations were losing huge chunks of advertising revenues to online competitors. Maybe it didn't matter that the company had a hotshot new CEO. How valuable could Tribune and Avon be if their business models were being undermined by a massive digital shift? What if the businesses I owned were not cheap because they were on sale—what if they were cheap because their futures were bleak?

Like everyone else, I had noticed the rise of the digital applications threatening my legacy holdings, but I had not studied them, largely because they were so expensive. Like most value investors, I scoffed at the high valuations that investors assigned these new-economy enterprises. Earlier in 2014, Facebook had paid $20 billion for WhatsApp, an instant-messaging company founded only five years earlier. Twenty *billion* dollars—that was double Avon's and Tribune's market value combined. But Avon and Tribune generated $10 billion in annual revenues between them, five hundred times more than WhatsApp.

Something is wrong, I remember thinking. Either this is the second coming of the dot-com bubble, or Facebook understands something that I and other old-economy investors don't. The value investor in me wanted to believe that the four most dangerous words in the English language remained "this time it's different." On the other hand, I had to admit that tech's rise didn't resemble the dot-com era fifteen years earlier. Tech companies were expensive—but maybe they were expensive for a reason. WhatsApp was on its way to 1 billion users, roughly 15% of the globe's population. Google generated $66 billion of search-related advertising revenue and continued to grow at a 20% to 25% clip. These and other digital applications had sound business models anchored by what appeared to be sustainable competitive advantages. Every year, they added more users, generated more sales dollars, and entrenched themselves more deeply into the daily lives of their customers.

Could I say the same for the companies I owned, which published newspapers, sold door-to-door cosmetics, and built freight cars? I could not.

Ever since Ben Graham introduced the discipline a century ago, value investing and technology stocks have not mixed well. They simply haven't fit any of our frameworks. A reversion-to-the-mean strategy doesn't work well because tech stocks nearly always look expensive relative to their historical averages. Software companies have few tangible assets and cannot therefore be valued using Graham's original asset-based analysis. Most importantly, value frameworks prize predictability and stability above all, and until recently tech stocks provided neither to investors.

Until recently, investing in "tech" meant investing in hardware—companies that manufactured PCs, routers, and fiber-optic cable. These businesses proved the wisdom of Buffett's advice never to confuse a growth industry with a profitable one. A company would introduce a new semiconductor or a new PC, and for a time the money would roll in; then competition would arrive, and profits would implode. The new millennium brought the beginning of better, software-based business models, but the technological infrastructure wasn't yet robust enough to sustain them. When tech stocks collapsed in the dot-com bust, it confirmed to value investors that the four most dangerous words in the English language were indeed "this time it's different." If there was any reversion to the mean in the tech sector, it was to the mean of chaos, and no serious value investor was interested in that.

Fifteen years later, however, something unusual happened. In 2016, Buffett, the guiding light of value investors and the keeper of the flame passed down to him by Ben Graham, bought $7 billion worth of shares in Apple. To say that this move mystified the investment community is like saying Catholics would be confused by a pope who opened the priesthood to women. Apple was a hardware technology company so historically brutalized by competition that in the late 1990s it was ninety days away from declaring bankruptcy. What, the value investing community asked itself, was the Oracle of Omaha doing?

Fortunately, I had a plane ticket to hear Buffett explain himself.

Every spring, 40,000 of value investing's faithful gather in Omaha, Buffett's hometown, to hear him and Charlie Munger expound on the state of their holding company, Berkshire Hathaway, and the world at large. Anyone interested in investing should make the pilgrimage to Omaha at least once: Buffett and Munger sit on a dais in a basketball arena and answer a full day of questions, laying out what they invested in over the past year and why. Even though Buffett is ninety-one years old and Munger's well past that, they remain committed to transmitting the lineage of value investing the old-fashioned way: orally and in person.

By the time I headed to Omaha in May 2017, I had begun to suspect that this time was indeed different. Google, Facebook, Tencent, and Apple were not the sketchy businesses of the dot-com boom. On the contrary, they possessed the same kind of brand loyalty and generational growth Buffett had spent his career looking for. And they were making money—lots of it. In 2016, Google's parent company, Alphabet, generated nearly $20 billion in net income. Coca-Cola, a longtime Berkshire holding that had been in business one hundred years longer, had made one-third of that.

By the time I went to Omaha, I'd sold Avon, Tribune, and the other stocks whose best days were behind them. I'd concluded that these companies were, in Wall Street parlance, value traps: cheap, but not valuable. My largest position was now Alphabet, my performance had improved, and my conversion to a new way of looking at the world was deepening. But it was still new, and I wanted to hear from Buffett why he'd bought Apple. Misery loves company, but so does conviction, especially when it's recently discovered.

Before the meeting, Buffett had explained to an interviewer how his Apple purchase didn't represent any material change from his methodology. He recalled the moment he realized that Apple possessed many of the same consumer franchise characteristics that companies like Coca-Cola did. When he took his great-grandchildren and their friends to Dairy Queen, he could hardly get them off their iPhones to order ice cream.

"I didn't go into Apple because it was a tech stock in the least," he would later say. "I went into Apple because I came to certain conclusions about the value of its ecosystem, and how permanent that ecosystem could be."

Onstage, Munger wouldn't let him off so easily. He teased Buffett about his latest big purchase.

"I think it's a very good sign you bought Apple," Munger told him. "It shows either one of two things. Either you've gone crazy, or you're learning."

The crowd laughed, because they understood that despite Buffett's protestations, what Munger said was true: Buffett buying Apple represented a dramatic change in his investment behavior. Throughout his seventy-year investing career—long enough to have children, grand-children, and great-grandchildren—Buffett had told his disciples in that polite Midwestern way of his that technology stocks weren't worth a value investor's time. Now here he was, plunking down $7 billion on Apple.

As the meeting progressed, it became clear that Buffett had been studying the digital economy deeply, and that he was impressed by what he'd learned.

"This is a very different world than when Andrew Carnegie was building a steel mill and then using the earnings to build another steel mill and getting very rich in the process, or Rockefeller was building re-fineries and buying tank cars and everything," Buffett told the crowd. "I don't think people quite appreciate the difference.

"Andrew Mellon would be absolutely baffled by looking at the high-cap companies now," he continued. "I mean, the idea that you could create hundreds of billions of value essentially without assets . . ."

"Fast," Munger interjected.

"Fast, yeah," Buffett agreed. "You literally don't need any money to run the five tech companies that are worth collectively more than two and a half trillion dollars in the stock market [Apple, Microsoft, Alpha-bet, Amazon, and Facebook], who have outpaced any number of those names that were familiar, if you looked at the Fortune 500 list thirty or forty years ago, you know, whether it was Exxon or General Motors, or you name it."*

Munger, who is almost always more direct than Buffett, chided both himself and his partner for not buying Alphabet, the parent company of Google.

"If you ask me in retrospect what was our worst mistake in the tech field, I think we were smart enough to figure out Google," Munger told

---

* As of this writing, four and a half years later, the collective market value of these five companies has roughly quadrupled to $10 trillion.

the crowd. "So I would say we failed you there. We were smart enough to do it and didn't do it."

Buffett agreed, recalling how Google had first appeared on his radar screen a decade earlier when GEICO, Berkshire's auto insurance subsidiary, began to buy Google Search ads on a per-click basis.

"We were paying them $10 or $11 a click or something like that," Buffett said. "Any time you're paying $10 or $11 every time someone just punches a little thing where you've got no incremental cost at all, that's a good business."

For someone who has trained himself to think in shades of gray, Buffett's overall conclusion about the rise of the digital economy was unusually black and white.

"This is a different world than existed in the past, and I think it's a world that's likely to continue," he told the crowd. "I don't think the trend in that direction is over by a long shot."

Aha, I thought. Buffett and I are on to the same idea, and the word is getting out. As the meeting ended, I found myself looking forward to talking about it with my peers at the dinners and cocktail parties that followed the gathering.

At these events, however, I found that nobody wanted to talk about Apple. Nobody, in fact, wanted to talk about tech in general or the new world that Buffett had just described. Instead, everyone continued to chatter away about the same old old-economy businesses they'd been chattering away about for years. They talked about Buffett's recent airline investments, even though these investments represented a smaller dollar commitment than the one he'd made to Apple. People also spent lots of time unpacking tiny, incremental changes Buffett had made to Berkshire's various insurance subsidiaries.

This struck me as insane. Both airline and insurance companies were the very kind of mature, capital-intensive businesses that Buffett had just said were fading away. Had nobody heard our guru telling us it was time to look forward rather than back?

In the winter of that year, I went to see Lew Sanders, the man with the ice-blue eyes who'd overseen Bernstein's black box when I was there. Lew's reckoning with the old ways had come earlier than mine, in the aftermath of the financial crisis of 2008–2009. Banking stocks had fallen when the housing bubble popped, and the black box told Lew that they were cheap. Relying on decades of successful experience with reversion to the mean, Lew bet heavily that financial stocks would come back. Many, of course, never did. Lehman Brothers went bankrupt, Bear Stearns was sold for cents on the dollar, and Citibank had to raise so much equity that more than a dozen years later it still trades at a tenth of its pre-crisis value.

By late 2009, the market had recovered from the crisis and the S&P was on its way to its best year in decades; Bernstein's flagship fund, however, remained down more than 50%. On another dark day in late December, Lew Sanders left his office at Bernstein for the last time.

I lost track of Lew after that, but he resurfaced for me as I began to wrestle with the ascent of the Digital Age. He had started his own firm, Sanders Capital, and I was shocked when I read that his top holdings included several tech companies, including Alphabet and Microsoft. Neither of these stocks was even close to attractive when viewed through traditional value lenses.

This made me very curious indeed. What had made the archbishop of reversion to the mean renounce it?

"Lew," I began, "over the last few years I've come to suspect that many of our old investing methods no longer work. Businesses like Alibaba, Facebook, and dozens of other, smaller companies are prospering. None look attractive when you look at them using conventional metrics—but maybe the conventional metrics are wrong. Maybe 'this time it's different' aren't the most dangerous words in the English language anymore; maybe it's 'life is going back to normal.'"

Lew was silent, and his ice-blue eyes were downcast. So I continued.

"I've begun to invest in such businesses," I said, "and I notice you're doing the same."

Still nothing.

"So, Lew, I have to ask you," I finally said. "What the hell is going on?"

Lew smiled, raised his glacial eyes to mine, and uttered four words that will remain with me for some time.

"The world," he said, "has changed."

CHAPTER 2

Value 1.0: Ben Graham and the Age of Asset Values

Ben Graham would have felt at home in the quiet, studious corridors of Sanford Bernstein. He and Kenny Abramowitz, the analyst whose shirttails flapped behind him as he hurried back from the bathroom to his desk, would likely have been good friends.

Although Graham became known as the father of modern security analysis, he was at heart an intellectual. He knew seven languages and routinely quoted Corneille in French, Kafka in German, and Homer in ancient Greek. Graham is likely the only financial analyst in history who, during a poor stretch of investment performance during the Great Depression, composed a poem about it. ("Where shall he sleep whose soul knows no rest," the poem concludes. "Poor hunted stag in wild woods of care?") Like many thinkers, Graham was known in equal measure for his brilliance and his absentmindedness. He invented a new version of the slide rule, but he would also often show up at work wearing two different-colored shoes.

Although he worked the night shift tabulating trucking statistics for a shipping company for much of the time he attended college, it took Graham only two and a half years to graduate second in Columbia University's class of 1914. The faculty regarded him so highly that upon graduation they offered him teaching positions in three different departments: mathematics, English, and philosophy.

But these positions paid only modestly, and Graham had a widowed mother and two brothers to support. His father had died when Graham was nine, and his mother had eked out a living in part by taking in boarders. When it came time to choose a profession, Graham chose the one that offered the potential for making the most money: finance.

The Wall Street that Graham entered in 1914 was hardly intellectual. On the contrary, it was a bizarre combination of carnival, casino, and amusement park ride. The Curb Exchange transacted its business literally on the curb of Broad Street, where every day the police would rope off a twenty-yard area for traders to buy and sell millions of dollars of securities. Many wore bright hats of differing colors so that their order clerks could identify them and use hand signals or simply shout instructions from the buildings above.

Graham was hired by a firm called Newburger, Henderson & Loeb, run by an imposing, gray-haired man named Alfred Newburger. "If you speculate, you'll lose your money," Newburger warned Graham on his first day. "Always remember that."

At the time, bonds were considered safe and respectable—for gentlemen—while stocks were for the sharpies on the curb. Newburger's best-paying customers, however, were the traders and speculators who emulated those sharpies, so even a New York Stock Exchange firm like Newburger, Henderson & Loeb was compelled to operate like a gambling hall. One of Graham's initial jobs was to collect the bets clients placed on the outcome of the 1916 presidential election. In the early twentieth century, it was legal for a Wall Street brokerage to function as a bookie.

Another of Graham's early jobs was to act as a "board boy," responsible for reading the ticker tape and chalking up the changing prices on a large blackboard. Every day, the brokerage's clients would congregate in what was known as the customers' room to watch the action unfold. This room was an important revenue center for Newburger, Henderson & Loeb, a sort of off-track betting parlor where gamblers could congregate and watch the horses run. The firm may have discouraged its employees from wild bets, but Newburger encouraged its clients to do so. That's where the money was.

In some ways, this indiscipline was understandable. When Graham began, there was little information available about publicly traded businesses. Today, the Securities and Exchange Commission requires listed companies to report their financial status every quarter, but the Securities and Exchange Commission didn't exist then. Today, a normal set of corporate financial statements runs to one hundred pages or more, but when Graham began, even the most prominent American corporations published only one-page balance sheets, which are snapshots of what a company owns and what it owes. Income statements, which today give investors details about a company's revenues and expenses, often contained only a single figure: the company's profit or loss for the year.

Despite his boss's warning, Graham fell under the speculative spell. He followed one of the customers' room regulars into buying the stock of a railroad that soon went bankrupt. Graham also lost thousands of dollars of his and his friends' money in an IPO called Savold Tire, which turned out to be a fraud. Afterward, Graham visited the man behind the Savold scheme, who admitted that he had duped investors. He placated Graham by settling with him for 33 cents on the dollar, and Graham only briefly considered filing criminal charges. The prevailing laws were so weak, and the regulatory and enforcement framework so poor, that he knew going to the authorities would do no good.

———

By 1920, Graham was a new father, and he needed to find a reliable way to make money, one that didn't involve speculation. As it happened, the years after World War I were the perfect time for someone with a mind like Graham's to begin searching for such a system. War demand had put the nation's industrial economy on a more stable financial footing, making companies like U. S. Steel and Amalgamated Copper inherently more reliable investments. These companies also began to produce more information about their operations after President Theodore Roosevelt empowered regulatory bodies like the Interstate Commerce Commission to require more disclosure from corporate America.

The young man who had tabulated trucking statistics to make a living while attending Columbia could now focus his mind on concrete financial data rather than odds on who would win the next presidential election. Studying the financial statements, Graham began to notice patterns. In 1915, he read the financial statements of Guggenheim Exploration, which was planning to dissolve itself by distributing its assets to shareholders. See below for the key part of Graham's balance sheet analysis.

Graham was struck by the disconnect between the first number and the last. While Guggenheim was trading for less than $69 per share, the sum of its parts totaled more than $76 per share. This meant that Guggenheim was trading for roughly 90% of its asset value. An investor could buy a share of Guggenheim for $69, then sell $76 worth of the stocks that Guggenheim owned. This would create a spread, in Wall Street terms, of roughly $7 per share, or slightly more than 10%.

This method was not speculation. This was analysis. Once Guggenheim liquidated itself and distributed its stockholdings to shareholders, a 10% return was virtually guaranteed. Following this logic, both Graham and members of his firm implemented the trade, and they made their spread when the dissolution proceeded.

Newburger and its principals, however, ignored most other such ideas that Graham brought them. Graham once suggested that New-

	Market Value September 1, 1915	
1 share Guggenheim Exploration		$68.88
Equivalent Securities Held		
.7277 share Kennecott Copper @ 52.50	=	$38.20
.1172 share Chino Copper @ 46.00	=	5.39
.0833 share Amer. Smelting @ 81.75	=	6.81
.185 share Ray Cons. Copper @ 22.88	=	4.23
Other assets	=	21.60
Total		$76.23

burger's clients dump the common shares of Consolidated Textile, a speculative favorite of the day, and buy the company's convertible bonds instead. The bonds were not only safer, Graham argued, they also offered current dividends and decent price appreciation potential. But the partners demurred; one explained that Consolidated's common stock traded much more frequently than its bonds, and the men in the customers' room liked to see its stock price constantly changing on the chalkboard. Everyone but Graham was surprised when the bonds appreciated, while the stock declined 70%.

In 1923, Graham quit Newburger, Henderson & Loeb to start his own investment operation. He was only twenty-nine but he had an edge, and he knew it.

"To old Wall Street hands it seemed silly to pore over dry statistics when the determiners of price change were thought to be an entirely different set of factors—all of them very human," Graham later wrote in his memoirs. But "[a]s a newcomer—uninfluenced by the distorting traditions of the old regime—I could respond readily to the new forces that were beginning to enter the financial scene. I learned to distinguish between what was important and unimportant, dependable and undependable, even what was honest and dishonest, with a clearer eye and *better judgment than many of my seniors, whose intelligence had been corrupted by their experience*" (emphasis added).

––––––––––

Although financial statements were being published more frequently, they were often not widely circulated, so Graham often had to travel to read them. One day in 1926, while in the record room of the Interstate Commerce Commission in Washington, DC, he discovered the company that would establish both his career and his reputation.

Northern Pipe Line was one of the smallest of the thirty-four companies created by the dismantling of Rockefeller's Standard Oil. Its only asset was a tiny pipeline that carried oil from the Ohio border fifty miles through Pennsylvania to the northeast corner of New York. But Graham wasn't interested in the pipeline's operations. As with Guggenheim, he was interested in the disconnect between the value of the company's assets and its stock price.

Northern Pipe Line owned $95 per share worth of high-grade railroad bonds; its stock, however, was trading for only $65 per share. What was a splinter of the mighty Standard Oil doing with millions of dollars of railroad bonds? Graham asked himself. Even more to the point, why was the stock trading at a roughly 30% discount to these bonds? The pipeline was profitable and required little capital to run. Indeed, Northern paid $6 per share in annual dividends. Why was the stock so inefficiently priced?

Back in New York, Graham went to see the Bushnell brothers, who ran Northern Pipe Line from Standard Oil's legendary offices on 26 Broadway. Graham told the brothers that he didn't think the company needed to own those railroad bonds. Wouldn't it be better, he asked them, to distribute $95 per share worth of bonds to the shareholders, who owned the stock at $65 per share? Wouldn't that unlock $30 per share of value while leaving the pipeline free to continue to make money and pay dividends?

The brothers told him that was impossible. Northern might need to sell the bonds and use the cash either to replace or expand the pipeline. When might that occur? Graham asked. The brothers said they weren't sure. When Graham persisted, the brothers became exasperated.

"Look, Mr. Graham, we have been very patient with you and given you more of our time than we could spare," Graham, in his memoirs, recalled. "Running a pipeline is a complex and specialized business, about which you can know very little, but which we have done for a lifetime. . . . If you don't approve of our policies, may we suggest that you do what sound investors do under such circumstances, and sell your shares?"

No, Graham told them. He was not going to sell his shares. He would, however, attend the company's next annual meeting and present his ideas to the company's other shareholders.

In January 1927, Graham took an overnight train to Pittsburgh, and the following morning, in a snowstorm, he took the trunk line to Oil City, the site of Northern Pipe Line's annual meeting. He found only eight people there: the two Bushnells, five pipeline employees, and himself.

The meeting was called to order, and one employee moved that the previous year's annual report be approved.

"Please, Mr. Chairman," Graham interjected. "Where is the annual report?"

"We are sorry, Mr. Graham," one of the Bushnells replied, "but the report won't be ready for several weeks."

"But Mr. Bushnell," Graham asked, "how is it possible to approve a report that isn't ready and available?"

After a brief, whispered conference between the brothers, one of them said, "We have always handled the matter this way. Those in favor say 'aye.'"

With the nonexistent annual report approved, the brothers moved on, and after a few more formalities, the chairman asked for a motion to adjourn.

"But Mr. Bushnell," Graham said, rising to his feet. "As we agreed in New York, I should like to read a memorandum for the record relating to the company's financial position."

"Mr. Graham," Bushnell replied, "will you please put your request in the form of a motion?"

Graham did so. Finding no seconds, the motion failed, and the meeting was over.

The following year, Graham came with four lawyers and the support of many other shareholders. While Graham had failed to secure the proxy of the Rockefeller Foundation, which owned nearly a quarter of Northern Pipe Line's stock, he had enough votes to elect two of the board's six directors. A few weeks later, back in New York, the Bushnells summoned Graham to their offices at 26 Broadway.

"You know, Mr. Graham, we were never really opposed to your ideas on returning capital to the stockholders," one of the brothers told him. "We merely felt that the time was not appropriate. As matters now stand, we are ready to present a plan which we think will meet with your complete approval."

And with that, Northern Pipe Line disgorged $70 per share in cash and securities. They also reorganized the company so that in the end, Graham's $65 per share investment nearly doubled.*

———————

When other former Standard Oil pipelines followed Northern and distributed excess capital to their shareholders, Graham's reputation, his bank account, and his self-confidence all grew. His asset-based approach was working well—so well that he used the securities he owned as collateral to borrow money and buy even more stocks with it. He leveraged up, as we say on Wall Street, or "went on margin," and he did this right into the Crash of 1929.

All stocks sank, and Graham's borrowings amplified his losses. By 1932, his investment partnership was down 70% from its peak. It would not be until five years after the crash that Graham's fund recovered to pre-1929 levels.

Graham moved his family to a smaller apartment, and his wife found work as a dance instructor. He abandoned the car and chauffeur he'd kept for his mother, but he did not abandon his investment discipline. While other investors despaired, Graham continued to invest using his asset-based system. He paid special attention to current assets, or the assets a company owned that could be easily sold for cash. A long-term asset like a factory may or may not fetch its balance sheet value when put on the market; current assets like inventory were more likely to sell for full price.

As with Guggenheim and Northern Pipe Line, Graham wanted to buy a company for less than it could be liquidated for, but the Great Depression caused him to be even more strict in his methodology. To be extra conservative, Graham applied a discount even to these cur-

————————————

* Only later did Graham discover the real reason the Bushnells had capitulated: Executives at the Rockefeller Foundation had favored Graham's plan, but they had not wanted to embarrass the brothers by giving Graham the foundation's proxy. In typical circumspect Rockefeller fashion, however, they had let their wishes be known, and Graham's plan was consummated.

rent assets. The resulting approaches came to be known as "net current asset value," or "net working capital," and to this day Graham's disciples like to hunt for what they call "net nets."

The stock market of the 1930s was so depressed that hundreds of securities met even such metrics. When Graham dissected White Motor Company's year-end balance sheet for 1931, he valued White's cash and securities at 100% of their book or carrying value, its receivables (what other companies owed White) at 80% of their carrying value, its inventory at 50%, and its factories at 20%. After subtracting all of the company's liabilities from this figure, Graham estimated that the liquidation value of White Motor Company was $31 per share—but the stock was selling for $8 per share. In 1932, Graham wrote a three-part series for *Forbes* entitled, "Is American Business Worth More Dead Than Alive?" in which he argued that more than a third of the nation's publicly traded industrial companies were trading for less than the net liquidation value of their readily saleable assets.

Graham had invented what would become known as value investing, or at least the first iteration of it. Focused on hard assets and a company's liquidation value, Graham's approach can be called Value 1.0.* Like all subsequent iterations of value investing, Graham's system was rigorous, disciplined, and, like the scientific method, both repeatable and verifiable. While Graham's full performance records do not survive, it appears that by using this system he outperformed the larger market by a comfortable margin from the 1930s until he retired in 1956. Graham estimated his returns to be 20% per year, roughly double the market averages over that period.

Not only was Graham a good investor, but he was also an open and generous teacher. He taught a course on security analysis at Columbia Business School for more than twenty-five years, and he wrote books that helped investors make sense of the markets. In the depths of the

---

* I am indebted to my friend and colleague Chris Begg, cofounder and chief investment officer of East Coast Asset Management, who gave me the terms Value 1.0, Value 2.0, and Value 3.0, which I use throughout the book.

Depression, Graham codified his philosophy in *Security Analysis*, a monumental textbook that introduced readers to his methods and ideas. Chief among these ideas was clearly distinguishing between investment and speculation. While a speculator buys a share of stock as a lottery ticket, an investor buys one to become a part owner in the actual business. Graham also encouraged investors to buy stocks only when they had what he called a margin of safety. Investing with a margin of safety means that you should buy a stock at such a low price that even if things go wrong with the business, not much happens to the stock.

Fifteen years later, in *The Intelligent Investor*, Graham introduced readers to another seminal idea: Mr. Market. Instead of treating the market as an abstraction, Graham suggested that we personify it. We should give the market a name and deal with it as we would a business partner. We and Mr. Market own shares of certain companies together, but we are business partners with different temperaments. While we try to remain levelheaded, one day Mr. Market shows up to work in a euphoric state, offering to buy our share of the business for an absurdly high price. Later, Mr. Market has veered from manic to depressive, and he offers to sell us the same share for an absurdly low price.

Although it sounds commonsensical today, in Graham's time the idea was revolutionary. Rather than be governed by Mr. Market's moods, we should take advantage of them. The stock market is an amalgamation of mostly irrational human beings and therefore tends to be crazy—but we don't have to participate in the insanity. Let others gather and shout at the curb; we will read the annual reports and remain rational.

The concepts of margin of safety and Mr. Market continue to be important conceptual tools that will never become obsolete, but Graham's specific valuation framework contains important holes and gaps.

Part of the problem with Value 1.0 is inherent in all successful investing strategies. As more people adopt the system, the excess returns get competed away. As you can see in the table below, the so-called value premium associated with buying stocks cheaply relative to their assets has largely receded.

There are deeper problems with Graham's system, however. Value 1.0 is largely a short-term strategy, one that requires a constant portfolio recycling as inexpensive stocks appreciate to fair value. Graham's approach came to be known as "cigar butt investing," because the stocks in a Graham portfolio are like cheap stogies picked up off the sidewalk. Good for only one or two puffs, they must be quickly discarded, then new ones found. It's time-intensive to find such stocks, track them, and decide on entry and exit points for each one. Because the recycling is rapid, gains in cigar butt investing are also often taxed at ordinary-income rates, which are higher than long-term capital gains rates. In the upper tax brackets, a 20% short-term investment gain becomes a 10% gain after paying 50% taxes on it.

Finally, and most importantly, Value 1.0 is rigid, rote, and monomaniacal in its focus on asset prices. As a result, the biggest fish routinely slip through its net. Value 1.0 was well-suited to its times; its strict adherence to numerical formulas kept investors away from speculating. It's a simple system with easy, binary answers: either a stock meets Graham's liquidation criteria, or it does not. Finding a company you can invest in with a margin of safety, Graham wrote in *The Intelligent Investor*, "rests upon simple and definite arithmetical reasoning from statistical data."

Value premium of the cheapest stocks over the most expensive stocks on a price/assets basis

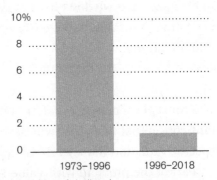

Source: Andrei Goncalves and Gregory Leonard, "The fundamental-to-market ratio and the value premium decline," Kenan Institute of Private Enterprise Research Paper, 2020.

As time went on, however, and the world emerged from the Great Depression, Value 1.0 appeared increasingly ill-fitted to the American economy. The United States became both more stable and more prosperous after World War II, and Graham's asset-based system didn't identify businesses whose value resided in their ability to generate large and growing income streams rather than in their net assets. Obsessed with formulas, Graham ignored any sort of qualitative analysis; one of his assistants recalled that he would get bored and look out the window if anyone started talking about what a company actually did. Likewise, Graham discouraged his analysts from meeting with a company's management. He felt the executives might dupe his analysts and distract them from the numbers, which were what really mattered.

Walter Schloss, who worked for Graham and later became a legendary value investor in his own right, once pitched Graham on a company that wasn't selling for a fire sale price but owned a promising new technology: Haloid, which would later commercialize the Xerox machine.

"Walter, I'm not interested," Graham told Schloss. "It's not cheap enough."

Graham's conversation with Walter Schloss about Haloid echoes the one he had a generation before with the partner who scoffed at the idea of trading Consolidated Textile common stock for its safer bonds. At the time, Graham had said his superiors' experience had corrupted their intelligence; one wonders if the same thing ended up happening to Graham. But if the previous generation's error had been recklessness, the central error in Graham's system was that not only was it doctrinaire, it was also overly cautious.

Graham retired early for a portfolio manager, at sixty-two. A wealthy man, he could afford to return to his earlier, more intellectual interests. He translated a novel from Spanish, published a volume of poetry, and began to split his time among the United States, Portugal, and Aix-en-Provence. Shortly before he died, however, Graham made a bizarre, indirect confession about the limitations of the discipline he had created.

The confession came in a two-page postscript from the final edition of *The Intelligent Investor*, published in 1973. Graham apparently felt so sheepish about the matter that he wrote of himself in the third person. He describes what transpired as if it had happened to someone else, whereas in fact it happened to him and his longtime business partner, Jerome Newman.

"We know very well two partners who spent a good part of their lives handling their own and other people's funds in Wall Street," Graham begins in the postscript. "Some hard experience taught them it was better to be safe and careful rather than to try to make all the money in the world. . . . In this way they did quite well through many years of ups and downs in the general market . . ."

Graham goes on to say that in 1948 he put 20% of his partnership's assets into a single stock. The stock was cheap relative to both assets and earnings, and, Graham writes, he and his partner were "impressed by the company's possibilities."

Almost soon after Graham bought it, the stock took off and continued to appreciate—so much so that over time, it made Graham and his partners two hundred times their initial investment. This appreciation quickly made it look expensive on Graham's asset-based metrics, but he decided to keep it because, as he says in his memoirs, he regarded the company as "sort of a family business."

"Ironically enough," Graham concludes in *The Intelligent Investor*, "the aggregate of profits accruing from this single investment decision far exceed the sum of all the others realized through 20 years of wide-ranging operations in the partners' specialized fields, involving much investigation, endless pondering, and countless individual *decisions*" (emphasis added).

In other words, a single investment in one great business made Graham more money than a generation's worth of cigar butts combined.

The company was GEICO, the automobile insurer. Yet in Graham's memoirs, he mentions GEICO only twice, once in relation to an insurance claim he filed with them. Northern Pipe Line, on the other hand, receives a whole chapter.

"Are there morals to this story of value to the intelligent investor?" Graham asks in the conclusion to his postscript. "An obvious one is that there are several different ways to make and keep money on Wall Street. Another, not so obvious, is that one lucky break, or one supremely shrewd decision—can we tell them apart?—may count for more than a lifetime of journeyman efforts."

Here, Graham was dissembling. By the time he wrote this postscript, he knew that identifying great businesses like GEICO did not involve a lucky break. He knew that the identification of great businesses could be systemized, just as he had systematized asset-based investing. One of his former Columbia students—his star pupil, in fact, the only one he ever awarded an A+—was proving it through his own investment track record.

CHAPTER 3

Value 2.0: Warren Buffett and the Brand-TV Ecosystem

In 1950, an awkward, gangly twenty-year-old from Omaha, Nebraska, named Warren Buffett walked into Graham's security analysis class at Columbia Business School. Building on the foundation that Graham had given him, Buffett would become a billionaire thirty-six years later. Two decades after that, he became the world's richest person, simply by investing.

Like Graham, Buffett had finished college early, and like Graham he was highly intelligent, analytical, and bookish. Buffett likes to joke that while his classmates were looking at *Playboy*, he was studying the S&P stock manual. In most ways, however, Buffett and Graham couldn't have been more different. Urban and urbane, Graham enjoyed the New York theater scene, traveled frequently, and spent many of his later years in Europe. Buffett was raised in the middle of the American prairie. He speaks only English, and his favorite meal is hamburgers. Aside from brief periods on the East Coast, Buffett has spent his entire life in Omaha enjoying a simple life of comfortable, mid-century American stability. After sixty-three years, he still lives in the same two-story home that he bought in 1958 for $31,500.

Like Graham, as a teenager Buffett was intrigued with technical analysis, which tries to predict the short-term movement of stocks by studying charts of how they've moved in the past. He quit that when he saw the charts looked the same when viewed upside down as right-side up. Then, in college, he read Graham's *The Intelligent Investor* and was struck by a force so powerful that he would later describe it in spiritual terms.

"I felt like Paul on the road to Damascus," he would tell an interviewer. "I don't want to sound like a religious fanatic or anything, but it really did get me."

Graham's system appealed to Buffett for the same reason it's appealed to generations of investors. It was a *system*, with strict dos and don'ts. Like a cookbook, it was formulaic and easy to put into practice. Take the assets on a company's balance sheet, discount them for liquidation, then subtract the company's liabilities and compare the net figure against the stock price. Buy only when the price is less than your calculated liquidation value.

Buffett also liked Graham's articulation of less quantitative investment principles. "Margin of safety" meant being careful—investing prudently rather than recklessly. The idea of Mr. Market made concrete what Buffett intuitively understood about human nature: when it comes to money, most people aren't rational. Because investors incline to alternating periods of exuberance and despair, the key to success is to train oneself to take the opposite side of wherever Mr. Market happens to be. As Buffett would later put it, the key is to be fearful when others are greedy, and greedy when others are fearful.

With the zeal of a convert, Buffett left Omaha for New York City so he could study under Graham. He wound up with a business school degree, but he didn't care about that. Buffett was there for one teacher alone, and he attached himself to Graham like Plato did to Socrates.

When Buffett returned to Omaha to work in his father's stock brokerage, he began to imitate his mentor's cigar butt investment style. As Graham had done with Northern Pipe Line, Buffett bought the Sanborn Map Company for the securities it owned, and then he agitated for management to disgorge them. Later, Buffett bought a controlling interest in the Dempster Mill Manufacturing Company, a struggling windmill maker in rural Nebraska whose stock was cheap relative to its asset value. He hired a new manager who cut costs and liquidated assets; Buffett made nearly three times his money when he sold the company two years later.

It soon became clear, however, that Buffett would diverge from his teacher's conservative, mechanical investment style. Surveying the United States from its geographic center in the 1950s, Buffett could see that the country was prospering. The war was won, and the Great Depression was receding as both an economic and psychic phenomenon. Buffett beheld a young, creative, and energetic nation that was the world's major economic superpower. Every year, its middle class became bigger and wealthier. Recessions and frauds remained, of course—they will always be with us—but both the stock market and the economy were advancing in relatively stable fashion. The wild speculations and the panics once so common in Graham's day were increasingly the subjects of amusing anecdotes from a different time.

Buffett, in other words, realized that the world had changed. He also realized that, as an investor, he needed to change with it.

Specifically, Buffett understood that in such a bountiful time he could and should focus on something besides Graham's fire-sale-asset values. He came to see that a company's profits correlated more closely with market-beating stock returns. He also realized that assessments of both the quality of the business and of the management team running it required more attention than Graham had paid them.

Buffett was heavily influenced in his thinking by John Burr Williams, an economist who had written a book called *The Theory of Investment Value*. Like Graham's *Security Analysis*, Williams's book had been written in the depths of the Depression, but it was as optimistic and as forward-looking as Graham's was cautious. While Graham looked at a business statically, as a collection of assets and what they could be sold for today, Williams focused on a business's ability to produce earnings and dividends over time. In accounting terms, Graham focused on the balance sheet, which was just a snapshot of a fixed point. Williams focused on the moving picture of the income statement.

Williams's major hypothesis was that the value of any business—any financial instrument, for that matter—is the sum of all its future profits, discounted back to the present. "Discount" in this sense means to reduce, or haircut, the value of any earnings figure except the current one. Because the future is unpredictable, every bird but the one in the hand is suspect. Thus, $1 of earnings in Year 1 is worth $1, but $1 of earnings in Year 2 might be valued at 90 cents, 81 cents in Year 3, and so forth.

This formula, which came to be known as discounted cash flow, or net present value, can become quite involved and technical. Fortunately, you don't need to understand its ins and outs, because discounted cash flow is useless as a practical investment framework. It's impossible to predict profits beyond a few years with any accuracy— and even if you could, small changes in the discount rate lead to large differences in net present value.

Such complications mean that Buffett and other sophisticated investors rarely project a company's cash flows. Instead, they use a business's current earnings relative to its current stock price as a rough yardstick to measure whether they're getting a good deal. The cheaper the stock price when compared to a business's current earnings, the thinking goes, the more attractive the opportunity. If a company is earning $1 per share and it's selling for $15 per share, its current price earnings multiple is fifteen times, but if it's selling for $10 per share, its multiple is lower and the price is therefore cheaper. Though formally known as the price/earnings multiple, this metric is such common shorthand on Wall Street that it's usually called "the P/E multiple," "P/E," or simply "the multiple."

Though unworkable as a practical model, Williams's idea of net present value is nevertheless a brilliant theoretical construct. Like Graham's ideas of margin of safety and Mr. Market, the idea of net present value concretizes what's intuitive to anyone with a grain of common sense: the more a company can grow its future earnings, the more valuable it is today. Graham's focus on liquidation value reveals nothing about a company's ability to earn money over time; simple mathematical calculations about a company's asset values don't help an investor determine which companies have a bright future and which don't. Finding such businesses does not involve certainty but probability: which businesses are more likely than others to grow and prosper. Such conclusions cannot be reached through a paint-by-numbers framework. They require *judgment*, and judgment is qualitative rather than quantitative.*

Buffett got to exercise such judgment early in his career when, in 1951, he studied GEICO, the auto insurer that Graham had kept holding even though it looked too expensive. When he'd finished his analysis, Buffett wrote about the company for the *Commercial and Financial Chronicle* in an article entitled "The Security I Like Best." It is a remarkable piece of analysis, if only because in it, Graham's twenty-one-year-old former star pupil doesn't once mention GEICO's assets or its liquidation value. Instead, Buffett focuses on GEICO's potential to grow and compound its earnings over time.

In 1951, GEICO was not the gecko-loving insurance giant we know today. It was a tiny auto insurer that, unlike most of its peers, targeted one specific customer group: people who worked for the government. (The name GEICO is an acronym for Government Employees Insurance Company.) Early on, GEICO's managers deduced that government employees were generally cautious people. As such, they were considerably less prone than others to car accidents, and this made GEICO's insurance pool inherently less risky than average. GEICO also decided to target such clients in an unconventional way. Rather than establish a large network of insurance salespeople, each of whom would have an assistant and an office, GEICO sold its policies using only the mail and the telephone.

While this direct approach reduced GEICO's reach, it increased its profitability. With no agents to pay and fewer accident claims than most, GEICO's operating profit margins were nearly 30%. As Buffett noted in his analysis, the average insurer in 1951 didn't reach 7%.

---

* For more, see John Burr Williams's *The Theory of Investment Value*. Alternatively, read Berkshire Hathaway's 1992 annual report, in which Buffett gives a condensed version of Williams's ideas.

GEICO's operating model was so lean, in fact, that it could earn these superior margins while offering policies at a 25% to 30% discount to the competition. This put GEICO in a very favorable position indeed. A generation later, in 1985, Harvard Business School professor Michael Porter would formally name this idea "competitive advantage." Buffett, the plain-spoken Midwesterner, saw it in less abstract terms. Agentless and targeting less risky drivers, GEICO had an *edge* that made it more likely to prosper relative to the competition in the years ahead.

In formal terms, GEICO's competitive advantage was that of a "low-cost provider." Every American who drives is legally required to buy auto insurance, but nobody wants to pay much for it. This dynamic makes car insurance a commodity, like sugar or cotton, and in commodity businesses the key determinant of competitive advantage is cost. Whichever company can sell the commodity at the lowest price will gain market share. As Buffett outlined in his article, GEICO's operating model made it the clear low-cost option for car insurance, and because it was such a small company, GEICO's growth was as close as you can get in business to a fait accompli. It operated in only fifteen states; in New York, which had some of the highest auto insurance rates in the nation, it had well under 1% market share.

In 1951, Buffett could not have predicted that GEICO would one day widen its target audience while continuing to use its direct-sales model to command nearly 15% of all American auto insurance policies. It was easy for him to conclude, however, that—given GEICO's competitive advantages—it would one day be multiples bigger than it was.

This kind of analysis was leagues away from Graham's "simple and definite arithmetical reasoning from statistical data." GEICO's investment appeal lay not in the onetime liquidation value of its assets; it resided in the business's ability to generate higher and higher profits for years to come.

Thus began a decades-long tug of war inside of the mind of Warren Buffett, a tug of war between the conservative, Depression-era framework of his teacher and the more optimistic, forward-looking perspective of John Burr Williams. The optimistic side got a strong helping hand in 1959 when Buffett met Charlie Munger, who would become Buffett's alter ego and business partner. Munger loathed Graham's cigar butt style of investing, referring to Graham's system over the years as "madness," "a snare and a delusion," and one that "ignored relevant facts." Munger preferred businesses like GEICO, which had obvious competitive advantages and thus a reasonable likelihood of a good, long run ahead.

With early successes like GEICO in his mind and with Munger in his ear, Buffett continued to explore and invest in companies whose main investment allure had to do with business quality rather than asset value. In 1963, he bought American Express, which dominated the market for both traveler's checks and credit cards. AmEx was a textbook call on postwar American prosperity. As it grew wealthier, the middle class spent and traveled more, and it trusted American Express to help them do so.

One of the places people were visiting was Disneyland, which in 1966 Buffett and Munger also visited. While their wives and children enjoyed the park, the two walked it and analyzed its economics. Disneyland had lots of tangible assets—what is the Dumbo the Flying Elephant ride except iron and steel?—but what struck Buffett and Munger was that the rides' real value had nothing to do with Disney's ability to liquidate them. On the contrary, their value arose from the connection that visitors made to the Disney movies and television shows on which the rides were based. Americans loved Dumbo and Davy Crockett and Alice in Wonderland, and their attachment to these characters deepened when they visited the park. With such a deep hold on customers, Disney could sell movie tickets, advertisements on its TV shows, admission to its theme parks, and merchandise associated with the characters. This capacity gave Disney an asset that was different than iron and steel. Buffett and Munger couldn't quantify it on a balance sheet, but they knew it was valuable.

In 1972, using their holding company, Berkshire Hathaway, Buffett and Munger bought one of their first wholly owned subsidiaries: See's

Candies, which made confectionery and ran a chain of sweet shops on the West Coast. As with Disney, the value of See's stemmed from the love customers felt for the product. Knowing how attached Western-ers were to See's Candies, after they bought the business, Buffett and Munger began to raise the prices, just like Disney did every year at its theme parks. In both cases, customers continued to pay.

"Interestingly enough," a thirty-seven-year-old Buffett wrote in a letter to investors, "although I consider myself to be primarily in the quantitative school, the really sensational ideas I have had over the years have been heavily weighted toward the qualitative side where I have had a 'high-probability' insight.' This is what causes the cash register to really sing."

The "high-probability" insight, of course, had to do with a busi-ness's competitive advantage—its edge. These edges were not always identical. GEICO had a low-cost competitive advantage, while Ameri-can Express, Disney, and See's all possessed a brand. What linked these companies together, however, was something about their business that allowed it to earn more money over time.

Buffett described this phenomenon as a "moat" around a business. In Buffett's worldview, every enterprise is a kind of economic castle, which in an open-market economy is vulnerable to marauders. Busi-nesses attack each other, trying to destroy their competition so they can plunder the profits inside their castle walls. The weapons they use are lower prices and constant product improvement, and usually the only real winner is the consumer—unless that company has a moat to keep competitors away. Only businesses with some sort of moat will prosper rather than merely survive.

"The key to investing," Buffett said in a 1999 speech that was later published in *Fortune*, "is not assessing how much an industry is going to affect society, or how much it will grow, but rather determining the competitive advantage of any given company and, above all, the dura-bility of that advantage."

As Buffett's experience with Disney and See's showed, brands had a special hold on Americans, and Buffett observed that much of that hold derived from the media ecosystem of the latter part of the twentieth century. Every night, millions of Americans tuned in to the evening news and then stayed tuned in to watch their favorite dramas and sitcoms. In return for this information and entertainment, Americans sat through nightly bombardments of advertisements. The nation's biggest brands, Buffett noticed, used this ritual to reinforce and extend their hold on the public's purchasing habits. Coke and Bud were first in consumer loyalty and market position, which meant they could spend more on advertising than their competition. Doing so allowed them to grind both mind share and market share upward. Buffett calls this kind of corporate behavior throwing sharks and alligators into the moat.

Buffett also observed that while there were many brands, there were only three major national networks: ABC, NBC, and CBS. This arrangement created what Buffett called a toll bridge, a metaphorical span over which every brand had to travel—for a fee, of course. This toll bridge gave the networks the same pricing power and generational loyalty that Disney and See's Candies had. Such dynamics also applied to local television stations and, especially, to newspapers. Often there was only a single publisher per metropolitan area, so Buffett bought shares in the Washington Post Company, and he bought 100% of the *Buffalo Evening News*. He also bought shares in Ogilvy & Mather and Interpublic, leading advertising agencies that served as the enablers of the brand-TV ecosystem.

In 1985, when he was fifty-four, Buffett made his biggest investment ever: Capital Cities, which owned dominant local television affiliates in obscure markets like Albany, New York, and Providence, Rhode Island. Media moguls had little interest in such unglamorous properties, but with his rational eye Buffett saw them for what they were: gold mines with almost no competition.

Because they were such good properties, and because they were well managed by an executive named Tom Murphy, whom we'll meet in chapter 6, Buffett paid up for Cap Cities. While the average stock was selling for ten times its current earnings in 1985, Buffett paid sixteen times more for Capital Cities, or 60%.

He knew that his former teacher, who had died nearly a decade earlier, would not have approved. "Ben is not up there applauding me on this one," Buffett told *Business Week*.

The Cap Cities transaction capped a twenty-five-year trend of Buffett paying higher and higher multiples for businesses he was convinced had an edge. From a strictly quantitative point of view, he should have been doing the exact opposite. The 1960s through the 1980s were a period of rising interest rates, and in such circumstances stock investors generally pay lower prices for stocks. When U.S. government bonds, the safest investment in the world, are offering higher yields, it makes little sense to pay up for stocks. But as the following chart shows, instead of paying lower prices for stocks as a multiple of current earnings through this period, Buffett paid higher ones.*

Why did Buffett pay up like this? Because he was becoming ever more confident that his system, which we can call Value 2.0, worked. In Value 2.0, business quality rather than price determines a superior investment. Price still matters, but eventually it's competitive advantage—the edge, the moat—that matters most. A bad business won't make a great long-term investment no matter how cheap it is.

While Graham's parsimony remained ingrained in him, Buffett saw repeatedly the truth of his new worldview. In 1972, when he and Munger were negotiating to buy See's Candies, they almost lost the deal by haggling over a $5 million difference in the purchase price. He needn't have worried: fifty years after he'd bought it, See's Candies had generated more than *$2 billion* in cumulative pretax profit.

This is the essence of Value 2.0. Over time, a good business's growing earnings stream overwhelms the "high" initial price you pay for it. Over time, business quality trumps price paid.

---

* The chart expresses the price Buffett paid as an "earnings yield," which is earnings divided by price rather than price divided by earnings. Because companies often don't dividend out their entire earnings, this metric is theoretical, but it's nonetheless helpful because it allows us to compare a stock's "yield" to a bond's yield.

Buffett Paying Up

Selected purchases versus government bonds

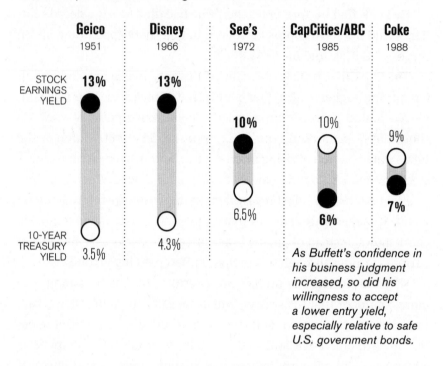

	Geico 1951	Disney 1966	See's 1972	CapCities/ABC 1985	Coke 1988

STOCK EARNINGS YIELD — Geico 13%, Disney 13%, See's 10%, CapCities/ABC 10%, Coke 9%

10-YEAR TREASURY YIELD — Geico 3.5%, Disney 4.3%, See's 6.5%, CapCities/ABC 6%, Coke 7%

As Buffett's confidence in his business judgment increased, so did his willingness to accept a lower entry yield, especially relative to safe U.S. government bonds.

By the early 1990s, Buffett's turn of the value investing wheel had made him a billionaire, and his philosophical break with Graham and Value 1.0 was complete. Not a revolutionary by temperament, he nevertheless wrote a letter to shareholders in 1993 that comes close to value investing's equivalent of Martin Luther's Ninety-Five Theses.

"Whether appropriate or not, the term 'value investing' is widely used," Buffett wrote. "Typically, it connotes the purchase of stocks having attributes such as a low ratio of price-to-book value, a low price-earnings ratio, or a high dividend yield. *Unfortunately, such characteristics, even if they appear in combination, are far from determinative as to whether an investor is indeed buying something for what it is worth ... Correspondingly, opposite characteristics—a high ratio of price-to-book value, a high price-earnings ratio, and a low dividend yield—are in no way inconsistent with a 'value' purchase*" (emphasis added).

By focusing on businesses with clear competitive advantages, Buffett put up a record that no one has come close to matching. A $10,000 investment in the S&P index in 1965, when Buffett began to run Berkshire Hathaway, would today be worth roughly $2.5 million, but that same investment in Berkshire Hathaway would *135 times more*—$335 million.

Buffett's record is so awesome, in the original sense of the word, that words and figures fail to capture adequately the size of the gap that Buffett put between himself and the averages. The chart below shows how a man from the prairies created a mountain, making the market averages look plain.*

Making a Mountain: Berkshire Hathaway vs. S&P 500
Growth of $10,000 since Buffett took over in 1965

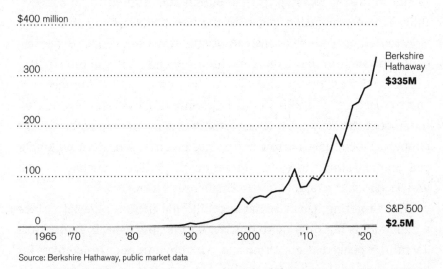

Source: Berkshire Hathaway, public market data

* Berkshire Hathaway's performance was supercharged by another key Buffett insight: if he owned insurance companies outright, he could invest the premium dollars in the stock market until it was time to pay out claims. Because his insurance companies consistently replace old premiums with new ones, the resulting "float" acts as a form of permanently borrowed money that Buffett can invest. And because his insurance companies have made a profit over the years, he has essentially been paid to use such leverage. Readers interested in learning more about this topic can read any of Berkshire's annual reports; Roger Lowenstein's Buffett biography also has a cogent discussion.

But times change, and when they change, investors must change with them. Buffett realized when he was young that what served the teacher no longer served the student. Today, there are ample signs that we should come to a similar conclusion.

In both its general worldview and its specific tools, Value 2.0 is beginning to fail us. As the economy changes, the moats that protect many of Buffett's classic postwar franchises are weakening. At the same time, Buffett's valuation framework, with its focus on mature companies generating lots of current earnings, hasn't captured the enormous value being created in the Digital Age. While Value 2.0 was exquisite in capturing where the money was, it's not capturing where the money is.

Let's begin with the first problem: the slow death of the brand/media industrial ecosystem that Buffett has hunted in so successfully. This deterioration began in the late 1980s, when cable television gained critical mass. Instead of only three networks, consumers could choose from more than one hundred channels and thus bypass the networks' toll bridge. Broadcasting gave way to what Munger calls "narrowcasting," the ability of niche channels like Home & Garden TV to target consumers open to advertisements for potting soil or hedge clippers. Since then, narrowcasting has given way to what we might call "monocasting," in which online media platforms such as Google and Facebook can target ads to a single user's tastes.

This targeting has eviscerated traditional media, especially since a digital ad is not only more precise, it's cheaper as well. Prime-time TV ratings peaked a generation ago, with obvious knock-on effects for local television. Meanwhile, the internet has destroyed the monopoly toll bridge that newspapers once commanded.

Mass brands, no longer able to rely on the nightly exchange between consumers and TV networks, are also losing their hold on the public. In a five-year period from 2013 to 2018, Johnson & Johnson's iconic baby products lost 10 points of market share, a shocking reversal in an industry where a single percentage point share gain or loss is considered material. Meanwhile, niche brands like Narragansett, a New England regional beer leveled by the rise of national television, are making a comeback. Younger people say the revival is because they like to buy local, and that may be true, but it's also true that younger people are no longer plugged into the Big Three TV networks. YouTube has more viewers under the age of thirty-five than do all other legacy television channels combined.

To their credit, Buffett and Munger grasped legacy media's disintegration some time ago. Aware that narrowcasters were burrowing under their broadcasters' moat, they sold their Cap Cities/ABC holdings in 1999. But the pair have been slower to recognize the secondary effects that media's decline has had on mass brands: Coca-Cola and Kraft Heinz remain large Berkshire positions. Buffett and Munger have been even more reluctant to abandon the financial-services industry, which Buffett first fell in love with when he found GEICO. A third of Buffett's top fifteen publicly traded stocks are financial-services companies, including American Express, Bank of America, and, until recently, Wells Fargo.

This is a real problem, because digital companies are looking at legacy banks the way a lion sizes up an aging zebra. Like GEICO, a bank's competitive advantages arises from its low-cost position. Unlike GEICO, however, which offers its customers better deals, banks have offered customers worse deals, betting—correctly, so far—that customers would put up with them. However, those days may soon be over.

Historically, a big bank has made the same kind of trade with its customers that a TV network makes. In return for news and entertainment, viewers give the network their attention during advertisements. With banks, customers get lots of physical branches and an array of financial products under a single roof: a checking account, a savings account, a home loan, and so on. In return, customers accept below-market interest rates on their deposits. In the past, the trade worked well for both parties. Banks get a cheap source of funds, which they can then loan out, while customers get a convenient way to bank. But from the consumer's perspective, the trade has always been negative.

To secure a cheap source of money, banks must in essence rip off their customers by giving them subpar interest rates. To perpetuate its competitive advantage, a bank is counting on people to be either too ignorant or too lazy to move their money to an institution that's willing to pay them more.

While it's true that it's hard to change banks when you have so many accounts with them, banks have abused their customers' trust for so long that they are all but inviting customers to leave. Not only do banks offer below-market rates, but they also routinely ding their customers with fees. Account-opening fees, account maintenance fees, fees for using another bank's ATM, fees for failing to maintain a minimum balance, overdraft fees—as anyone who has seen them on their monthly statement knows, the list is long. The average American pays roughly $20 in banking fees every month, more than they pay for a Netflix subscription. But at least, with Netflix, people get something.

Economists call this kind of behavior, in which one party extracts value from another without offering anything in return, "rent seeking," and while it's not illegal, it's usually not sustainable, either. The pandemic has shown people that they don't need a physical branch to conduct their business; meanwhile, digital challengers are offering financial products that are cheaper, faster, and better. So-called fintech companies, financial-services businesses that were born online, can approve home loans in half the time a brick-and-mortar bank can. Online companies are also offering rates on deposits that are *twenty-five times higher* than a legacy bank.

The old television network ecosystem is dying, mass brands are moribund, and legacy financial companies have exposed themselves to digital competition through their own bad behavior. Many of these companies, however, look cheap when viewed through the lens of their current price/earnings multiple. But they aren't cheap because they're attractive; they're cheap because their future is bleak. Meanwhile, tech companies look expensive on a current P/E basis, but they have generated and continue to generate tremendous wealth for their shareholders.

Why is that? What is it about value investing as currently constructed that lets most tech companies slip through its net?

The answer is complex, but I think it begins with Buffett's worldview. Buffett's career coincided with a time when the American economy was unusually stable and homogenous. In 1900, Washington, DC, had more than one hundred newspapers; by 1974, it had only one, the *Washington Post*, and Buffett was a major shareholder. By the end of the 1950s, clear leaders existed in soap (Ivory), gelatin (Jell-O), beer (Budweiser), and cola (Coke). These leaders took incremental market share simply by outspending their rivals on everything from advertising to distribution. New entrants—"disruptors"—hardly stood a chance.

Because the business landscape of the latter part of the twentieth century was so static, Buffett learned that successful investing consisted of identifying dominant, mature franchises that could slowly but surely grind sales and earnings higher. New growth industries like electronics and personal computers were born during this time, but few companies in them possessed an edge. Sales would boom for a brief period, but then competition would arrive, and everyone's economic castle would be ruined. As a result, Buffett was forced to choose between companies with lots of growth but no moat and more mature companies that had one.

Buffett's only major tech holding is Apple, which, although technically "tech," is in many ways just as he described at that 2017 Berkshire meeting I attended: a new variant of an old-time consumer products company. The iPhone is a beloved everyday product that dominates the high-end smartphone market, which—like the markets for cola, beer, and soap—is largely mature. Just about everyone in the world who's going to buy an iPhone has bought one, so Apple won't sell many more units beyond replacement ones. It will, however, continue to dominate the high end of the smartphone market, and it will use its platform status to grind profits and earnings higher.

Unlike many other tech companies, Apple is relatively unambitious in terms of trying to attack new markets; as a percentage of sales, Apple spends only about one-third of what Alphabet, Microsoft, and Facebook spend on R & D. Over the last decade, the company has acted like an old-fashioned capital allocator, using much of its cash flow to repurchase its own shares in the open market.

Most tech companies, however, aren't mature like Apple. Dozens, even hundreds of businesses trade in the public market today that possess both moats and exponential growth prospects. This happy confluence is not something Buffett and Munger are used to seeing. Experience has taught them to look for steady, persistent economic farmers, safe behind their moats and castle walls. The blitzkrieg success of companies like Alphabet, Facebook, and Netflix is alien to them, and little wonder. They'd never seen anything like it until they were more than seventy years old.

Even the metaphors that Buffett and Munger use to describe competitive advantage suggest the anchored, immobile way they view the world. Buffett likes "moats," which are used to defend against a siege. Munger talks about looking for companies that are "entrenched," implying that he prefers a competitive dynamic in which one side is well dug in and in no rush to move.

Today's economy, however, is as dynamic as the postwar world was fixed. For most tech companies, now is not the time to dig in and settle down behind a moat. Now is the time to reinvest and grow.

CHAPTER 4

Value 3.0 and the BMP Checklist

It's funny: what led me to conclude that tech is where the money is, and that value investing needs to change in order to see it properly, had nothing to do with technology or a tech company itself. It was instead an old-economy company in one of the most boring industries you can imagine.

This company makes generic spare parts for airplanes. Like GEICO in 1951, it has a small share of a huge addressable market. Like GEICO, its competitive advantage stems from being the low-cost provider of an essential product. Even its name resembles GEICO's: It's HEICO, a company I came across during my wretched period of underperformance in the mid-2010s.

At the time, I was working with a talented analyst named Clint Leman. I asked Clint to write a simple computer program that used different metrics from the "look for cheap stocks" criteria I'd been using. No longer would I put price ahead of business quality as I had with Avon, Tribune Media, and the rest. Instead, I would search for businesses with superior economic characteristics, then see about price later. I also asked Clint to screen for management quality using a single simple yardstick: whether executives owned a lot of stock in the company they were running.

Clint's screen turned up a dozen names, the most interesting of which was HEICO. The company was founded in 1957 as Heinicke Instruments Company, but the story really begins in the late 1980s, when one of Larry Mendelson's kids stumbled upon it.

Larry Mendelson was a New Yorker who, while attending Columbia Business School a decade after Buffett, took the same security analysis course Buffett had. After graduation, Mendelson moved to Florida and made a lot of money in real estate, but he put his value-investing skills to work in the stock market as well. In the 1980s, his sons Eric and Victor attended Columbia as undergraduates; while they were there, Larry asked them to look for undervalued securities in their spare time. Interest rates were falling, stocks were modestly priced, and Larry was looking for a business he and his sons could take over and run. In keeping with Ben Graham's tradition, the Mendelsons didn't particularly care what the business did. It just needed to be cheap, poorly managed, and located in Florida, where the family wanted to stay.

One day, while doing research in the Columbia law school library, Victor found HEICO, which appeared to meet the family's criteria. The company specialized in making medical-laboratory equipment, but it had made a series of acquisitions, including one in the aerospace business. By the time Victor found HEICO, it had been public for nearly thirty years but barely made any money.

Like Graham with Northern Pipe Line and Buffett with Sanborn Map, the Mendelsons saw HEICO as a company whose shares they could buy in the open market and then agitate for change. Unlike Northern Pipe Line and Sanborn Map, however, HEICO's appeal lay not in the liquidation value of its assets, but in the latent earnings potential of its aerospace subsidiary.

Several years before the Mendelsons came upon HEICO, an engine on a Boeing 737 had caught fire during takeoff in Manchester, England. Fifty-five people died, and authorities later determined that a malfunction in one of the engine's combustion chambers caused the fire. Regulators ordered airlines around the world to replace these combustors at regular intervals, beginning immediately. When the component's manufacturer, Pratt & Whitney, couldn't meet the surge in demand, half of the world's 737s were grounded.

Because HEICO had been authorized by the Federal Aviation Administration to make a generic version of this combustor, business was brisk when Victor came upon the company. What intrigued the Mendelsons, however, was not the one-off combustor demand—that would soon taper off—but the idea of using HEICO as a platform to produce hundreds or even thousands of generic spare parts for the airlines.

Current management was doing nothing to exploit the opportunity, but to the Mendelsons the market appeared vast. Unlike the auto industry, in which generic components can be sold without any regulatory approval, every airline part must be blessed by the Federal Aviation Administration and similar international bodies. If the FAA had approved the generic manufacture of a critical jet engine part, the Mendelsons asked themselves, why wouldn't it approve other, less critical parts? And if HEICO secured such approval, wouldn't the airlines be interested in an alternative source for spares? Original equipment manufacturers like Pratt & Whitney and General Electric enjoyed monopoly or near-monopoly positions in almost all their replacement parts: like so many companies, they were abusing their power by engaging in rent-seeking behavior. Rather than innovate their way to increased profitability, GE and the rest raised prices far above the rate of inflation and, lacking an alternative, the airlines had no choice but to pay.

As they learned more about airline spare parts, the Mendelsons discovered that HEICO could produce and sell a generic option at a 30% to 40% discount and still make healthy profits and returns on capital. The Mendelsons also found that there were few patents or intellectual-property rights attached to aerospace replacement parts. Moreover, the market for spares was huge—it's roughly $50 billion a year today—and the aerospace industry was growing. Like American Express, investing in airline travel is a classic call on rising worldwide prosperity, which leads to a rising demand for travel.

In 1989, the Mendelsons and their allies bought 15% of HEICO's stock in the open market. After a proxy fight almost as ludicrous as Graham's Northern Pipe Line contest, they secured four seats on the board and named Larry Mendelson the new CEO. He immediately sold HEICO's lab business and focused on the market for airplane spares.

The early going, however, was hard. It was clear that HEICO had a low-cost advantage over branded manufacturers, and in theory the FAA and the airlines loved a cheaper alternative. In practice, what Buffett calls "the institutional imperative" got in the way. From the perspective of an FAA bureaucrat, the calculus went something like this: if I approve this part for sale, the upside is that the airlines save some money—but if a plane using a part I approved goes down, I do, too. The calculus for an airline purchasing manager was the same. As a result, for nearly a decade, only a few, non-critical parts were approved for manufacture each year. But like my friend Alex with his Apple investment, the Mendelsons didn't lose conviction in their initial thesis for HEICO. Realizing that the perception of safety was the main obstacle, the Mendelsons focused on producing parts of the highest quality, and in 1997, Lufthansa vindicated their conviction when it bought a 20% stake in HEICO's spare-parts subsidiary. As part of the deal, Lufthansa began to order generics in bulk.

Business got a lot easier for HEICO after that. German engineers had signed off on HEICO's products. What more did the other airlines need to know?

When Clint's screen led me to HEICO in 2015, it had shipped 68 million parts without a single adverse incident, and nineteen of the world's top twenty airlines bought parts from the company. For a generation, sales had grown 16% a year and profits had grown 18% annually, both multiples above the average American company. As so often happens with great businesses, HEICO's low-cost moat has been augmented by a secondary one: with a 30-year track record of safely producing generic spares, HEICO has earned the trust of both the airlines and the FAA. Any other company wanting to scale up in the generic market would have to spend a decade or two earning that same trust. In the formal language of competitive advantage, this creates a barrier to entry to any other company tempted to compete against HEICO.

HEICO's moats are large and deep, and as the chart below shows, its stock has compounded at 23% per year for thirty years. A $10,000 investment in the S&P 500 index beginning in 1990, when the Mendelsons took over HEICO, would be worth $200,000, but that same amount invested in HEICO would be worth $5 million—twenty-five times more. Peter Lynch was right: superior companies succeed, and investors over time are rewarded accordingly.

Despite this spectacular rise, HEICO today still has less than a 5% market share of aftermarket spares. After a generation in the business, HEICO now makes 10,000 generic parts, or one-half of 1% of the 2 million total parts on a plane. At its current rate of introducing seven hundred new parts annually, it would take HEICO 3,000 years to produce all those parts in generic form. Even if you took a conservative view and said that 75% of the parts were too complex to ever be genericized, it would still take HEICO seven centuries to manufacture the rest.

Running such calculations in 2015, I felt the same way Buffett must have felt when he found GEICO in 1951. Like GEICO, HEICO had a sustainable low-cost competitive advantage. Like GEICO, HEICO had a tiny share of a large and growing market. And, perhaps best of all, HEICO's edge, like GEICO's, did not come from cynical rent seeking. On the contrary, both HEICO and GEICO used their low-cost positions to offer customers a better deal. In both cases, customers saved money and shareholders got rich.

After finishing my work on HEICO, I knew that I was done with stocks like Avon and Tribune Media, whose main virtue was that they were cheap. My reversion to the mean and my cigar butt asset value days were also over. Except in times of extreme market stress, no longer would I value businesses with recourse to what they could be liquidated for.

I vowed to be a loyal Buffett/Value 2.0 disciple. But as I studied the software-based business models of Alphabet, Amazon, and the rest, I

Total return since the Mendelsons took over HEICO

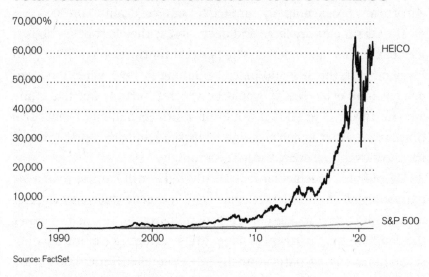

Source: FactSet

began to wonder: Did I have to settle for the kind of mature, battleship franchises that Buffett favored? Before the software revolution, businesses like HEICO and GEICO, which had both moats and exponential growth potential, were rare. Thanks to the rise of the digital economy, however, they're now relatively common. It occurred to me that, unlike Buffett and his generation of value investors, it was now possible for me to hunt for companies that possessed the same three qualities that GEICO and HEICO possessed:

- A low market share . . .
- . . . of a large and growing market . . .
- . . . with a clearly identifiable competitive advantage that will allow the company to grow sales and profits for years to come.

Once I wrote these attributes down, it all seemed so clear. For most of his career, Buffett had been forced to choose between mature, moated companies on the one hand and immature, vulnerable companies on the other. But I could have both.

Does a company I'm studying have a low market share of a large and growing market, and does it have a durable edge? The former gives the company exponential growth potential; the latter gives it a moat. Asking these questions now represents the foundation of what I call Value 3.0, and I don't need a computer program to help me to answer them. I simply pursue my normal research process, reading about companies online and in newspapers, magazines, and books. I study companies' financial filings, I listen to their investor presentations, and I talk to my circle of contacts on Wall Street and in business. If the company I'm reading or hearing about doesn't possess both competitive advantages and exponential growth opportunities, I'm not interested. If they do, I'm like a pointer dog who's just caught the scent of his prey.

Business quality—moats plus exponential growth—has become the major part of my system, but it's not the only one. Like Buffett, I've noticed that a business's performance depends considerably on the executives who run it. This revelation hit me with force when I studied HEICO. In my experience, many corporate executives are more interested in maximizing their own wealth through their salaries, perks, and stock options than they are in working to maximize long-term shareholder value. The Mendelsons aren't this way. They have a vision for the company and time to execute it. Larry Mendelson has been CEO of HEICO for more than thirty years, and he's not in any hurry to retire; when he does, his sons will likely take his place. The family also own nearly 10% of HEICO's shares, which means, in Wall Street parlance, that they eat their own cooking.

"I make $1 million a year in salary," Larry Mendelson told me once, "but if HEICO stock goes up $1 per share, my family makes more than ten times that. What do you think I care about more, my salary or the stock price?"

Listening to Larry Mendelson talk this way led me to articulate the first critical question regarding management quality: Do the managers think and act like owners—or are they just hired hands, interested in skimming from the people who own the ranch?

It's not enough, however, to merely want to act like an owner. Before they can act like one, managers must understand certain key principles about what drives long-term shareholder value. These drivers include financial concepts such as Williams's net present value and metrics like return on capital. While these ideas are not difficult to grasp, you'd be surprised how few executives grasp them. The chief financial officer is often the only senior executive who's really internalized them, and he or she is usually a quiet, analytical type like the ones that roamed the halls of Sanford Bernstein when I was there. Most CEOs, on the other hand, got where they did through a healthy dose of ego, charisma, and what John Maynard Keynes called "animal spirits." Once in the corner office and running a large organization, it's unlikely they'll adopt a rigorous financial mindset.

The Mendelsons couldn't be more different. They were investors in HEICO before they were its managers; they had analyzed the company before they began to run it. Because of this, the Mendelsons display a certain dispassion toward their company. They love HEICO and have made it their life's work, but they are not in love with it. They know that HEICO is merely a vehicle to deliver two main products: savings for its customers and wealth for its owners.

"HEICO is not in the aerospace business," Larry regularly tells investors. "We're in the business of generating cash flow, and that cash flow just happens to come from the aerospace business."

It's rare to find companies run by such people, but that only underscores how important it is to look for them.

After thinking through these issues, I found that I had two management quality questions to add to my three business quality questions.

- **Do the managers think and act like owners?**
- **Do the managers understand what drives business value?**

Armed with these filters—three on business quality and two on management quality—I had the beginnings of a template, a checklist I could use to help me tease out compelling Value 3.0 opportunities. Putting the questions down on paper, I saw how they could keep me focused on the three critical drivers of stock price performance: the quality of the *business*, the quality of the *management*, and the *price* the market is asking us to pay.

I call this template my BMP checklist, short for business, management, and price. You'll see it produced below. In my experience, if we get these three variables right, we will make solid, market-beating investments. If we get them wrong, we'll make mistakes.

———

Careful readers will notice several things about the BMP template. First, each question must be answered either "Yes" or "No"; like software, the system is binary. Second, business quality, the *B* in BMP, gets a disproportionate weighting. Business quality has always been the most important component of long-term stock performance, but it's especially important today. Driven by Moore's law, the software revolution has created a clear divide between those who will prosper in the Digital Age and those who will languish. If we are to succeed as investors, we must focus on the former and avoid the latter. Business quality is certainly more important than management quality. As Buffett has said, "When a management with a reputation for brilliance tackles a business with a reputation for poor fundamental economics, it is the reputation of the business that remains intact."

You may have also observed that I've not talked yet about price. That's intentional. I've saved price for last, because price is simultaneously the most important and the least important part of the BMP checklist.

Price is the least important factor in Value 3.0 because allowing it to drive our research process is allowing the wrong dog to lead the hunt. Price was the lead dog in Value 1.0; Buffett rightly rejected it as the lead dog in Value 2.0; and Value 3.0 rejects it, too. A price-first mindset

Business Management Price (BMP) Checklist

1 BUSINESS QUALITY   CHAPTER 6

Does the company have a low market share...?

...In a large and growing market?

And a sustainable competitive advantage?

2 MANAGEMENT QUALITY   CHAPTER 7

Does management think and act like owners?

Do the executives understand what drives business value?

3 PRICE "The Veto Question"   CHAPTERS 8 AND 9

Can you arrive at a reasonable earnings yield—ie, over 5%?

Yes As they say on Wall Street, back up the truck. If you're right on B, M, and P, you're in for a good long ride.

No Wait for Mr. Market to give you this business at a better price.

	YES	NO
Small share = lots of room to grow.		
Small share + large ultimate market = decades of opportunity ahead.		
If a company has an edge, it's almost inevitable that it will grow from a small player into a larger one. As it does, this "moat" will allow it to earn outsized profits without the risk of being disrupted by competitors.		
How management spends the company's money says a lot about whether they're interested in working for shareholders or for their own enrichment. Similarly, how they handle a company's stock with regard to acquisitions, buybacks, and options is telling.		
A company's leaders must understand the core business first, but executives like Buffett and Bezos also understand what drives economic value. Such executives tend to do best for shareholders.		

TOTAL

BMP SCORECARD	
4 or 5 out of 5	**Could be a great long-term holding. Proceed to PRICE.**
3 out of 5	**Wait and watch. "Nos" could become "yesses."**
0 to 2 out of 5	**Likely not candidate for long-term investment. Reject.**

directs us to businesses not because they are good but because they are cheap. Put like that, it seems obvious that giving primacy to what a stock's trading for is a strange way to try to build long-term wealth. Good businesses grow over time; isn't it better to own them?

Price, however, is also the most important variable in Value 3.0, in that while it merits only one question on the checklist, it's the veto question. Graham was wrong to let price drive his investment decisions, but this error is trivial when compared to Graham's insistence that we triangulate between price and value. "What am I getting in return for what I'm paying?" remains the central girder of any value-based investment framework. At some point, even the best business is overpriced.

Thus, after I've finished looking at the business and the management team, I look at the price the market is asking me to pay. If I can't get to a 5% earnings yield, I won't make the investment. Such a yield, otherwise expressed as a twenty times multiple on earnings, is a healthy but not outrageous price for a great business in today's low-interest-rate environment. If I can't buy the business for twenty times or cheaper, I'll wait and watch for Mr. Market to give me the opportunity.

In this way, my single price question functions in relation to business quality and management quality in the same way that Abraham Lincoln was said to have functioned in relation to his cabinet. If everyone voted aye but Lincoln voted nay, the nays had it.

I've already discussed the first difference between Value 2.0 and Value 3.0, which is a difference in outlook. The Digital Age is permitting us an even more optimistic and expansive worldview than the one implicit in Buffett's Value 2.0. Today, we can invest in companies that possess not only competitive advantages but exponential growth potential as well. The second crucial difference between the two systems concerns the specific variable of price, and the specific methodology we should use to measure price paid versus value received.

When the business landscape is relatively stable and static, as it was in the second half of the twentieth century, using current earnings is an appropriate way to answer the question, "What am I getting versus what am I paying?" Mature companies such as Budweiser, Coca-Cola, and Wells Fargo don't have to spend enormous sums to build out their businesses. Already entrenched, they can sit comfortably behind their economic moats and harvest the fruits of their competitive advantage. What such companies are earning today is therefore a reasonable proxy for their ability to generate profits going forward.

Of course, companies like Coke and Wells Fargo continue to spend on product development, sales and marketing, and distribution. Such spending, however, is nowhere near the levels we can observe in digital companies. Coca-Cola spends less than 30% of its annual revenues on sales, marketing, and research and development—but Intuit spends 45%. The difference, roughly 15 percentage points, is greater than the net profit margin of an average American business. The contrast is even starker when we consider companies with less ambition and global reach than Coke. Campbell's, the venerable American soup maker, dedicates only 12% of its revenue to sales, marketing, and R & D expenditure, about one-fourth of what Intuit spends.

As the above statistics suggest, digital companies such as Intuit are spending aggressively to exploit future opportunities. That spending distorts their profit-making ability in both the short and long term, and serious investors need to spend time thinking about the implications of such distortions.

Because its raw materials are non-physical zeros and ones, a software company is inherently three to four times more profitable than the average American corporation. It's common to see software companies report 90% gross margins, a profitability metric that counts only direct production costs. Even after factoring in all their expensive engineers and other related items, mature software companies such as Oracle, which operates at scale and doesn't reinvest much in its future, generate operating profit margins that approach 50%. Coca-Cola, one of Value 2.0's most powerful business models, generates margins that are roughly half that.

However, most software companies don't report anywhere close to

50% margins. Their inherent superiority as business models is therefore obscured.

Why is that? There are two discrete explanations.

The first has to do with how accounting rules distort the current reported earnings for most tech companies. As is the case with Intuit, R & D and sales and marketing expenses are usually a digital enterprise's largest expense line items. They are to the Digital Age what factories and inventory were to the Industrial Age: the engines that power corporate growth. But current accounting convention requires American corporations to immediately expense nearly all R & D and sales and marketing costs. Hard assets like property, plant, and equipment, however, can be expensed over many years. As a result, today's rules artificially depress reported earnings for tech companies, especially when compared to old-economy companies.

Because this is somewhat of a technical issue, I'll save an exploration of the accounting distortions until chapter 7, when I deal explicitly with corporate earnings. The larger and more conceptual point is that tech companies could report dramatically higher current earnings if they wanted to. It's just not in their best interest to do so. Early in their life cycles and with only a fraction of their markets conquered, digital businesses are in growth rather than harvest mode. They are wisely spending dollars today that will likely be worth more in the future. Such spending makes the E in the P/E ratio look small and the multiple of current earnings look large— but that is a misleading and deceptive snapshot of reality.

It's especially misleading when we are comparing tech companies, which are reinvesting heavily in the future, to legacy companies, most of which are not. To compare Amazon's or Alphabet's current profits to Wells Fargo's is like comparing an apple orchard in the springtime to an apple orchard in the fall: the latter is ready for harvest, while the former is just beginning to grow. If we are to be intellectually honest and analytically accurate, we must acknowledge that, while current earnings represent a good proxy of a mature company's ability to produce wealth, they are a poor proxy for a young digital enterprise's ability to do the same.

Finding a good proxy for a tech company's true earnings power is a difficult exercise, and there is no such thing as a precise answer. However, if we are capture the value that Amazon and Alphabet and all the rest have created and will continue to create, we must try.

To begin such an attempt, let's return to the Campbell's-versus-Intuit example. The two companies are well paired. Both are market leaders in their categories, and because their annual sales volume is roughly the same, spending differences cannot be explained by economies of scale, in which a larger company can spend less as a percentage of sales simply because it has more sales dollars to work with.

When I looked at Intuit in early 2020, it traded for nearly fifty times current reported earnings. Campbell's traded for only twenty times. This meant that my Year One earnings yield for Campbell's was 5%, but only 2% for Intuit. Optically, Intuit was much more expensive. But was it really?

Campbell's is the archetypal mature company. Its soups were an icon of the postwar world, but Chicken Noodle and its stablemates have been falling out of mainstream American consciousness for roughly a generation. To counteract sales declines in its core segment, Campbell's has diversified into snacks. It owns the Pepperidge Farm brand of cookies and Goldfish, and several years ago it bought Snyder's of Hanover pretzels and Lance crackers. Despite these acquisitions, Campbell's annual sales have grown at a less than 1% annual rate over the last decade. The company has numerous headwinds against it. Walmart and Kroger, which together account for roughly 30% of its sales, squeeze Campbell's every year for price and promotional discounts. The company's fatty, high-sodium products are generally considered off trend, and Campbell's can no longer count on the television network ecosystem to convince consumers that its soups are "M'm! M'm! Good!"

This state of play explains why Campbell's spends only 11% of its revenues on sales and marketing and only 1% on R & D. Campbell's markets are mature at best, so spending money to try to grow them would be foolish. It's wise for Campbell's to restrain itself.

Intuit is in the opposite position. It has grown sales 9% a year over the last decade, and its fastest-growing product, QuickBooks Online, is growing 30% to 35% annually. Given such dynamics, Intuit spends nearly 20% of its sales on R & D and nearly 30% on marketing. Such expansiveness is just as wise as Campbell's restraint. Intuit estimates that QuickBooks Online is used by only about 1% of the customers for which it's suited: of course Intuit should spend money to improve the product and reach more customers.

In short, Campbell's has a moat but no growth, while Intuit has both. This makes Campbell's a Value 2.0 company and Intuit a Value 3.0 company. Decisions about how much Intuit should spend on sales and marketing and R & D are difficult ones, but they're good choices to be faced with.

Like most tech companies, Intuit understands that they should make decisions not to maximize current profits but to maximize future ones. Intuit's management knows that R & D and marketing outlays are not expenses, as accounting rules would have us believe. They are investments. Even though they depress reported earnings, it's in Intuit's best long-term best interests to make them. Internally, Intuit requires that managers must see at least a 50% return on any marketing expenditure. Any rational businessperson would spend $1 today to make 50 cents in the future, but the financial statements show us only the $1 in expense. The 50 cents in future profits cannot be seen, only imagined.

This raises an important question: Should we penalize companies like Intuit because they forgo $1 of profit today to generate 50 cents tomorrow? Or do we acknowledge that this spending is smart, and do we thus adjust Intuit's earnings to make them comparable to companies like Campbell's, which doesn't have the luxury of such choices?

I think that the answer is clearly the latter. If we want to make a true, apples-to-apples comparisons between the two companies, then we must adjust one or the other's income statement. We should either load up Campbell's with Intuit's expenditures or lighten Intuit's spending so that it mirrors Campbell's.

If we do the latter and put the company into harvest mode, Intuit's earnings explode. If it were run like Campbell's, all the virtues of Intuit's nearly costless raw-material business model would remain, but the heavy spending on marketing and R & D would disappear. Of course, so would much of Intuit's revenue and earnings growth. Without all those marketing and product development expenditures, Intuit would be in the same position as Campbell's: mature and maximizing its current profit-generating ability. For our analytical purposes, that's exactly where we want Intuit to be.

The table that follows shows the results of this exercise. If we adjust Intuit's spending levels to Campbell's spending levels, Intuit's P/E multiple falls from forty-three times to twenty times. Its earnings yield would thus be 5%, the exact same multiple as Campbell's.

In truth, its earnings yield would be much higher, and its multiple much lower, because in a few years, Intuit's earnings are likely going to be 50% greater than they are today. I'll cover this important point more in detail in chapter 8.

Companies like Intuit trade at what first appears to be an unattractive multiple of current earnings, but this is a false appearance. Intuit's adjusted earnings, not its reported earnings, more realistically depict what I call its earnings power. So when I say that my veto price is anything above twenty times earnings, I don't use current, reported earnings for new-economy companies. I use earnings power.

Earnings power is neither a profit forecast nor an earnings estimate. Instead, *earnings power attempts to quantify a digital company's latent, underlying ability to generate profits*. By using earnings power rather than reported earnings, I hope to achieve several related goals:

- In the short term, to put tech companies on a directly comparable basis with more mature companies.

- To remove accounting distortions and "de-penalize," so to speak, a tech company's decision to invest for the future.

- In the longer term, to serve as a rough but directionally accurate proxy for a digital enterprise's ultimate ability to produce wealth.

———————

I'll explore earnings power in detail in Part II, which is the guts of the book. Part II contains a chapter on business quality, which will help you identify competitive advantage in the early twenty-first century. It also contains a chapter devoted to the other two main drivers of business value: the quality of the management team and the price the market is asking you to pay. Because it's such an important part of the Value 3.0 framework, earnings power gets its own chapter, too.

Part II concludes with case studies that walk you through how I used the BMP template to evaluate two tech companies in real time. It's interesting to theorize about what makes a superior investment in the Digital Age, and it can be intellectually stimulating to think about different valuation paradigms. But in this age or any other age, theorizing doesn't build your wealth. Putting theory into practice does.

Intuit vs. Campbell's

Because Intuit and Campbell's have the roughly the same revenues, we can compare them on a "common size" basis, which sets revenues at 100% and considers all costs as a percentage of sales. From this, we can see that:

Intuit has an inherently better business than Campbell's...

...Selling for the same price on an apples to apples basis

2020 Fiscal Year	Campbell's	Intuit		Intuit adjusted
Sales	100%	100%		
Cost of goods	65%	18%		
Gross profit	**35%**	**82%**	→	**82%**

Campbell's cost of goods includes chicken and tomatoes. Intuit's consists of zeros and ones. Intuit thus has 50 percentage points more gross margin dollars to deploy into marketing and R&D.

				Intuit adjusted
Marketing expense	11%	27%		*11%*
R&D expense	1%	18%		*1%*
Total marketing/R&D	**12%**	**45%**	→	*12%*

Using its greater gross margin dollars, Intuit spends nearly 4x more than Campbell's in marketing and R&D.

I adjust Intuit as if it were run as a mature company like Campbell's, not investing in the future...

Administrative/other	10%	9%		*9%*
Operating income	**13%**	**28%**		**61%**

. . . However, because Intuit has no cost of goods, its overall profit margins are more than twice as high.

...this makes its margins four times higher...

EPS	$2.50	$6.92		*$14.92*
Stock price	$50	$300		*$300*
P/E multiple	**20x**	**43x**		**20x**

...and its P/E multiple identical to Campbell's.

Source: company SEC filings

85

PART II

Tools for Picking Winners

CHAPTER 5

Competitive Advantage Then and Now

Because business quality is the main driver of long-term investment performance, if you want to succeed in the stock market, you must become an expert in identifying what makes a company superior. Identifying superior businesses depends in turn almost entirely on identifying a business's competitive advantage, which is the subject of this chapter.

Capitalism is an intensely competitive system; it sets market participants against one another, all of whom want to make as much money as possible—the "profit maximization" motive. To accomplish this goal, companies strive to please those who buy what they're selling. They lower prices, they introduce new products, they create new brands, and they innovate in any number of ways—all to outdo their rivals. To those who have never seen this battle up close, capitalism can seem like a rigged system in which everyone gets rich except those who deserve it the most. The truth, however, is much closer to *Hunger Games* than to *Easy Street*. Most companies resemble a hyper-aggressive basketball team that uses its elbows freely, routinely trips the other team's players, and would gouge the other team's eyes out if it weren't for a referee. Government has many important functions in our society, but when it comes to business, this is government's main function: to be the ref. Absent a referee to regulate them, businesspeople would destroy one another, and likely the planet, in pursuit of profits.

Because the competition is so intense, businesses that possess a durable competitive advantage are rare. Most are merely average; with nothing special to distinguish them from their rivals, they never truly grow and prosper. An average company grows in line with the growth of its underlying market, and below-average companies languish and eventually die. Only those businesses that possess an edge can produce more profits for their shareholders over time.

Nobody's ever added up all the competitively advantaged companies in the world, and the list is always changing as edges sharpen and dull, but my guess is that less than 10% of all companies have one. Their scarcity is what makes them so valuable, and so worth hunting for.

Recall from chapter 4, when I introduced the BMP checklist, that I've trained myself when searching for superior businesses to look for the following trifecta of factors:

- A low market share . . .
- . . . of a large and growing market . . .
- . . . with a clearly identifiable edge over the competition that will allow the company to grow sales and profits for years to come.

The first two qualities can easily be determined by both amateurs and professionals. On their investor relations website, companies will often tell you what they believe the size of their addressable market is and what they believe their share of it to be. Go to Intuit's site and you will see that Intuit now has 5 million online subscribers to QuickBooks, its small-business accounting product. Intuit says that the worldwide addressable market for QuickBooks is 800 million customers. Five million divided by 800 million equals less than a 1% share—I'm interested.

Such figures are easy to find even when companies don't publish them. For Amazon, we have the numerator but not the denominator to calculate its share of the total North American retail market. Amazon reported $236 billion in North American sales in its 2020 annual report; if you Google "U.S. retail sales 2020," you will find that the National Retail Federation reports that total U.S. revenues were $4.1 trillion. Canada's analogous site says that its retail sales were $600 billion, for a total of $4.7 trillion in North American retail sales. Amazon's $236 billion in sales divided by $4.7 trillion = 5% market share.

This is all straightforward. The question on business quality, however, is markedly more difficult. Does the business have a sustainable competitive advantage? What's its moat, and can the moat withstand the trials it will undergo as competitors try to breach it? As Buffett learned when he diverged from Graham, answering that question requires judgment, and you cannot find judgment online.

The good news is that judgment in the investing world is often mere common sense girded with a framework to help you organize your thoughts. As analysts, we can identify different kinds of competitive advantage. Then we can determine if the companies we're studying conform to any of these taxonomies. We can classify businesses by type in the same way that an ornithologist classifies birds.

Fortunately, many fewer types of competitive advantage exist than do bird species. Some are as old as commerce itself. Others, while not new, arise only during times of technological change, like now.

DON'T CONFUSE A FAST-GROWING COMPANY WITH A GREAT ONE

We'll begin by identifying what does *not* constitute a competitive advantage. As Buffett said in *Fortune*, rapid growth does not equal an edge, and conflating the two is a common mistake that both momentum and growth investors make. It's also one of the principal reasons these strategies tend to underperform.

Focusing too much on a company's near-term growth rate can in fact be disastrous. I once had a client who was desperate for me to buy stock in Vonage, a company that went public in 2006 after pioneering the business of routing telephone calls over the internet. Studying the market, I quickly concluded that nothing prevented other companies from imitating Vonage. The company had no moat to protect its economic castle. Its technology wasn't faster than the competition, its costs weren't lower, and Vonage's customers didn't care about the brand of the company that routed their calls over the internet.

I dissuaded the client from investing—and a good thing, too. After going hyperbolic for a time, Vonage's revenues and profits imploded once competitors entered the market and drove down prices. Three years after Vonage came public at $17 per share, it had lost more than 95% of its value. Fifteen years later, in late 2021, Vonage sold itself to another telecom company for a price that was 25% higher than when it went public. That's an annualized appreciation rate of 1.5%, which is hardly the sort of return required to beat the market.

GoPro is a more recent and even more egregious example of confusing a hot product with a sustainable business. GoPro, which makes handheld action cameras, went public in 2014 at a valuation of $3 billion. Investors fell in love with the idea that people could video themselves in all sorts of selfie situations, and GoPro's valuation doubled; unfortunately for GoPro and its investors, competitors also fell in love with the idea. The market became viciously competitive, and as the chart below shows, GoPro lost 85% of its peak valuation and has never recovered. With not much to differentiate itself from the competition, there's little hope it ever will.

Such examples prove Buffett's dictum, "Never confuse a growth industry with a profitable one." You should be especially mindful of this warning if you're thinking about investing in a tech hardware company: hardware is much more easily imitated than software. In truth, however, you should always keep Buffett's maxim in mind, because it applies to both tech and non-tech companies. Take the airline industry. Exposed to the same favorable tailwind of rising worldwide air travel that HEICO, Disney, and American Express enjoy, passenger airlines have nevertheless lost more money over their hundred-year history than they've made. Why? Because Delta, United, and the rest never gained a real edge over one another. None of the airlines possess a compelling brand, and none operate at a consistently lower cost than

GoPro's share performance since its IPO

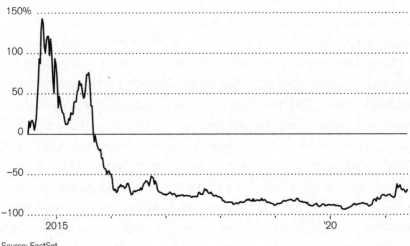

Source: FactSet

the competition. Lumped together in mediocrity, the airlines have done what all average businesses do: compete to serve the customer and give nearly all the gains to them. Occasionally, the airline industry turns a profit, and occasionally the story that "this time it's different" makes its way around Wall Street. Every time, however, the airlines begin to compete on price again, and profits again go in the tank. As is so often the case, the ultimate winner is the consumer.

MOAT 1.0: LOW-COST PRODUCER

Even though they're household names, Delta, American, and United have all gone bankrupt at least once in their history. HEICO, meanwhile, an obscure niche of the airline works in business but has grown its stock price five hundred–fold over the last generation.

How can that be? Through a low-cost advantage, one of the oldest moats around.

In commodity markets like corn, sugar, and steel, being the low-cost producer is the only advantage a company can hope for. People don't care much about the brand of corn or steel they're buying; beyond a certain base level of quality, they care about what it costs. As a result, whichever company can produce a commodity product more cheaply than its competitors will win a disproportionate share of the market. This law is immutable, like the laws of gravity or thermodynamics.

Here, the term "commodity" should be understood to include not just physical goods but anything consumers buy that is differentiated mainly by price. Shoppers don't go to Walmart because they love the experience; they go to Walmart because the company acquires everything from beer to broccoli more cheaply than its competitors and then passes those savings on to customers. Many industrial companies gained low-cost status simply by expanding faster and establishing bigger factory footprints than their competitors. Because they sold more widgets than their rivals, they were able to lower their unit costs, which gave them a low-cost edge. Great businesses like U. S. Steel, Ford, and General Motors were created in this way.

The Digital Age has altered many competitive dynamics, but in the early twenty-first century being the low-cost producer is more important than ever. When Walmart began to expand in the 1980s, customers had to drive to its stores to discover it had lower prices than the competition; when e-commerce began, it was possible to comparison shop without leaving your living room. Instacart allows you to shop for groceries from home and pit Kroger against Wegmans, Publix, and the rest. Google and Orbitz give you full and instant intelligence as to who's got the best deal on flights and hotel rooms. And while the internet introduced the world to radical price transparency, the smartphone perfected it. Now when you're in a Best Buy store, you can look on your phone and see if anyone can beat its prices.

Most tech companies, at least those powered by software, do not derive their competitive advantage from being a low-cost producer. Google and Orbitz don't give you the cheapest plane fare from New York to Cancún; it leaves that to the airlines. Tech companies' moats spring from phenomena like first-mover advantage and network effects, which we'll explore later in the chapter.

MOAT 2.0: BRANDS

With its automation and its mass production, the Industrial Age brought rapid gains in productivity, standards of living, and leisure time. What it took away, however, was the intimacy and familiarity people had with much of what they used in daily life. When Europeans and Americans lived on farms, they made their own clothes, their own cheese, and even their own liquor. Meat didn't come from the supermarket; it came from the animals you raised and slaughtered yourself.

As millions of people left the farm for the factory, however, they ceased such activities and started buying meat, cheese, and liquor from stores. Absent firsthand knowledge of what they were eating and wearing, they began to rely on manufacturers with reputations for quality. They began to rely on brands.

One of the first products to be sold on a mass, branded scale was soap, both for washing clothes and for personal hygiene. In the early nineteenth century, Procter & Gamble and Colgate began as soap companies. They were preceded by Pears, a company that's now forgotten but whose story illustrates how branded companies can construct a moat that allows them to grow profits for generations.

A Cornwall farmer's son, Andrew Pears moved to London as a young man in the late 1780s to become a barber's apprentice. Soon he opened his own shop in Gerrard Street and, as a sideline to barbering, began to sell cosmetics to wealthy Soho residents. Pears found that his makeup was often used to hide skin damage caused by soaps his customers had used that contained arsenic or lead. Sensing a market opportunity, Pears created a translucent bar scented with rosemary and thyme so that it smelled like an English garden.

Pears quickly became the must-have soap for the wealthy, but the real breakthrough came in the second half of the 1800s, when Thomas Barratt became head of the company and figured out how to sell it to the masses. When Barratt died in 1914, Pears was a household name among the growing middle classes in both the United Kingdom and the United States, and Barratt had become widely acknowledged as the father of modern advertising. Barrratt was one of the first people both to understand the power of trust in a brand and to exploit it systematically. "Good morning. Have you used Pears' soap?" was an early Pears tagline that remained a popular English catchphrase well into the twentieth century. To search for the new face of Pears, Barratt used kiddie pageants, which generated publicity itself, and in the 1880s, he hired the actress Lillie Langtry to hawk his soap. When a *Punch* cartoonist lampooned her sponsorship by portraying a bum saying, "I used your soap two years ago, and have not used any other since," Barratt used the parody as part of Pears' next marketing campaign.

Such methodical creativity earned Pears the loyalty and affection of the growing number of people who could afford its product. Although Pears made its soap with nothing more than glycerin and herb-scented rosin, Barratt knew that it would be foolish to sell Pears as a commodity. He rejected the low-cost producer route, knowing that there was much more money to be made strengthening customer loyalty to the Pears brand.

This bond allowed Pears to charge multiples of what the soap's inputs cost. Later, accountants who struggled to assign a value to this intangible connection between a customer and a brand called it "goodwill"; as the developed world became wealthier, other ingenious merchants extended the idea of goodwill from necessities like soap to nonessential items like soft drinks. John Stith Pemberton, wounded during the Civil War and later addicted to morphine in a military hospital, began marketing Coca-Cola as a curative for ailments as varied as indigestion, impotence, and drug addiction itself. Coke's main ingredients are sugar and water, but the company has habituated consumers to believe that Coke is "the pause that refreshes" and "the real thing." For decades, brands like Sam's Cola from Walmart have tried to undercut Coke on price, but people refuse to switch. They're in love with that red can and that curvaceous glass bottle.

Understanding this, Buffett bought Coke stock in 1988, and he continues to hold the shares more than thirty years later. "Coca-Cola is associated with people being happy around the world," he told students at the University of Florida in 1998. "You tell me that I am going to do that with RC Cola around the world and have five billion people have a favorable image in their mind about RC Cola, you can't get it done. You can fool around, you can do what you want to do. You can have price discounts on weekends. But you are not going to touch it. That is what you want to have in a business. That is the moat."

Today, enough people in the world make enough money so that power brands extend even to companies that sell nonessentials. Is a Hermès pocketbook or scarf worth $25,000? Yes—if the clever people in Hermès's marketing department work their magic well. "Our business," Hermès CEO Axel Dumas once told *Forbes*, "is about creating desire."

Desire is a powerful emotion, and many durable and valuable businesses have been built upon it. Hermès was founded in 1837 and has a market value of $140 billion; Coca-Cola began in 1886 and has a market value of $260 billion. Tiffany, founded in the same year as Hermès, puts mainly commodity jewels into a box the color of a robin's egg and sells them for a huge markup. LVMH, one of Hermès's rivals, recently bought Tiffany for nearly $16 billion, nearly three times more than the market value of Vonage and GoPro combined.

It's important for you to realize, however, that most brands don't last as long as Tiffany, Hermès, or Coke. Brands are as fickle as the people who fall in love with them, so as moats go, the branded moat is among the most vulnerable. The story of Pears soap shows us how a brand gets built, but it also shows us how one disintegrates. After Barratt's death, Lever Brothers bought the firm; in the hands of a conglomerate, Pears gradually lost both share of mind and of wallet in the UK and in the United States. It is all but forgotten in these countries, and its main market is now India, where it is that nation's fifth best-selling soap.

Pears, Revco, Borden, Cream City Brewing, Virgin Cola, Juicy Couture—the list of dead or moribund brands is much longer than the list of extant ones. Before you invest in a company whose main competitive advantage is its brand, you should therefore be convinced that the brand has staying power. A low-cost commodity business can continue to lower prices and widen its moat, but brand companies have no such levers to pull. Like Blanche DuBois, they rely on the kindness of strangers.

This is especially true today, when the television ecosystem that sustained mass-market brands for much of the latter part of the twentieth century is dying. Johnson & Johnson is losing market share to The Honest Company, founded a decade ago by actress Jessica Alba. New companies are using channels like TikTok and YouTube to scale up and challenge legacy brands with astonishing rapidity and ease. The Nelk Boys, a group of twenty-something young men who film pranks they perform as they travel across North America, have nearly 7 million YouTube subscribers. They sell almost $100 million of Nelk Boys apparel every year and are contemplating extending their brand to include men's grooming products, a chain of fitness studios, and a line of condoms.

The biggest brands today, however, belong to big tech. According to *AdWeek*, the world's top five most trusted brands are Google, PayPal, Microsoft, YouTube, and Amazon. A tech company's brand power, however, is arguably much stronger than one that relies on fads or consumer tastes. Google isn't marketing a status symbol or a fizzy drink; it's marketing a reliable search engine that consumers have become habituated to in their daily lives.

Because a tech company's brand has nothing to do with creating desire, it's more likely to endure. As long as a software company continues to deliver value to its customers, it can rely on actual experience rather than perception to sustain its hold on consumers. "We hold as axiomatic that customers are perceptive and smart," Amazon CEO Jeff Bezos wrote in his 1998 annual letter, "and that brand image follows reality and not the other way around."

PLATFORMS AND SWITCHING COSTS

When a company becomes the trusted, go-to application for search, e-commerce, social media, or any of the other new industries that have been born in the last generation, consumers tend to gravitate toward it en masse. This standardization becomes a source of competitive advantage itself. In the jargon of Silicon Valley, such products and services become platforms, allowing the company not only to earn money on its core business but also to introduce more profitable lines.

Apple is a classic platform company. The iPhone began as a relatively low-margin hardware device; it costs a lot to make them. The apps Apple sells on the phone, however, cost Apple nothing. The developers spend the money to build the app; for the right to sell it to more than 1 billion iPhone users, developers then pay Apple 30% of the revenue they generate.

You should be on the lookout for companies that have transformed themselves, or have the potential to transform themselves, into platform companies. To use a military simile, platforms are like aircraft carriers—huge, powerful staging areas from which a company can launch new attacks. Some, like Apple, are obvious, but others aren't. Roku began as a humdrum seller of gadgets that consumers use to stream Netflix and other channels at home, but it's used its dominant market share to force streaming channels to share some of their profits. I missed Roku, but I might have caught it had I been watching the market with my platform filter on.

Many digital enterprises want to become platform companies for the same reason banks want to sell you multiple financial products: the deeper a company gets its hooks into you, the harder it is for you to leave. In business school parlance, the switching costs are high, and these switching costs constitute a corollary competitive advantage to becoming a platform company.

So many people are accustomed to using Microsoft's Word and Excel, and have archived so many documents in both, that changing would cause months of agony. Anytime you spot this kind of sticky relationship between company and consumer, your antennae should go up. Like a brand, switching costs bind a consumer to a product—but, like a low-cost position, switching costs are more substantive than brands. Customers hate to change once they're comfortable with a product.

Once customers get used to a product, the drawbridge over the moat goes up, and it's fair to say that the drawbridge is up in any number of digital sectors today. Whether it's Apple with mobile phones, Google in search, or Intuit in small-business accounting software, tech has gone through its early dot-com spasm and reached what innovation scholar Carlota Perez calls a "bedding-in" period. Consumers have now become so accustomed to tech applications they like and trust that this cozy relationship will prove very, very hard to disrupt. This is true even when actual switching costs aren't high. It's not hard for people to change from Google to Bing—but the psychic switching costs are huge. People are used to Google, and it works. Why would they switch?

FIRST MOVERS AND FAST MOVERS

The term "first-mover advantage" comes from chess. The player playing the white pieces always begins the game and thus takes the initiative. Black responds, and usually it's white that's on the front foot the entire game. The same is true in business. In a new market, whoever stakes first claim to the territory often gets the best land, leaving the competition to settle for second best.

In times of slow technological progress and change, being the first mover is often enough to establish a durable competitive edge. During the Great Depression, a 3M engineer named Richard Drew invented Scotch Tape. Despite its enormous mass-market potential, innovation was so feeble after the crash that no company tried to imitate and improve upon 3M's product. With no competition, Scotch Tape remained the market leader even though 3M made no material improvements to the product for more than thirty years.

Can you imagine a modern company creating a new product, leaving it unimproved for more than a generation, and remaining the market leader? In today's economy, a company that doesn't continually innovate won't stay on top for thirty months, let alone thirty years. This is especially true since the advent of the Digital Age, when the pace of change is brutally fast. In times of technological transformation, speed and innovation matter much more than in times of stasis. That's why

Mark Zuckerberg's motto has been to move fast and break things, and it's why Elon Musk has adopted a launch-first, upgrade-later business model for both Tesla, his electric vehicle company, and SpaceX, his rocket company. Musk and his fellow entrepreneurs are much more comfortable with the land rush metaphor than they are with those of trenches and moats. "I think moats are lame . . . ," Musk said in 2018. "[I]f your only defense against invading armies is a moat, you will not last long. What matters is the pace of innovation."

Bankrupt now, Sears had a prosperous hundred-year history because it was the first mover twice in a century. In the late 1800s, Richard Sears and Alvah Roebuck noticed that general stores in rural America were abusing their monopoly position by charging high prices for poor-quality merchandise—another example of rent seeking. With mail service improving, Sears and Roebuck began to send rural residents a catalogue filled with various goods at affordable prices. They centralized distribution in a vast Chicago warehouse filled with the latest technology, including a series of vacuum tubes that allowed clerks to route orders to the right part of the facility. Then, after World War I, when the economy began to shift from rural to urban, Sears decentralized, building a network of department stores that thrived for more than fifty years.

Sears didn't invent either the mail order catalogue or the department store, so technically it wasn't the first mover in either business. It was, however, the quickest and the most aggressive in both. For this reason, "first-mover advantage" is perhaps better described as "fast-mover advantage." HEICO wasn't the first to make generic airplane spare parts, but the Mendelsons were the first ones to act urgently on the opportunity.

While it's useful to look for such urgency, you should be careful not to rely on a first- or fast-mover advantage to sustain your investment thesis. Being the first mover may establish a competitive advantage, but it will never perpetuate one. HEICO, GEICO, Amazon, and others have all established secondary advantages—a low-cost position, a trusted brand, an extensive distribution network—to supplement their first- or fast-mover advantage. Although Musk pooh-poohs moats, he has used Tesla's early lead in electric vehicles to build not only customer loyalty but also a low-cost position as well. Because it makes more electric cars than anyone else, Tesla's unit production costs are 25% lower than the industry average.

NETWORK EFFECTS

There is one final source of competitive advantage, and in many ways it's the most powerful of them all. Its name, network effects, captures the dynamic and energetic state of the early twenty-first-century economy.

Venmo, which is owned by PayPal, is a great example of a company that enjoys network effects. A decade or so ago, Venmo moved fast to build technology that allowed people to access their bank accounts from their smartphones and quickly pay one another. Somehow, Venmo developed a loyal initial following, a nucleus that began to exert a gravitational pull on others. The more people joined, the more it encouraged others to join. I got the app after enough friends said "Venmo me" when we were splitting a restaurant bill or settling up Yankees tickets.

The old-fashioned term for network effects is "virtuous circle," although tech people prefer to call it "the flywheel effect." A flywheel is a circular device that dates back to the Stone Age. It was used as the driver of the earliest water-powered mills and then later refined for the steam engines of the Industrial Age. A flywheel is heavy, so it's difficult to get it going, but once it begins to spin, the flywheel is equally difficult to stop. "Each turn of the flywheel builds upon work done earlier, compounding your investment of effort," business author Jim Collins writes. "A thousand times faster, then ten thousand, then a hundred thousand. The huge heavy disk flies forward, with almost unstoppable momentum."

WhatsApp, whose purchase by Facebook in 2014 confounded me

that gloomy New Year's Eve, possesses this kind of flywheel, or network effect. So does Airbnb. Hard-pressed to pay their rent in New York City, Airbnb's founders started offering their apartment to tourists. Like the Mendelsons with HEICO, the early going at Airbnb was hard, but the company gradually found other apartment dwellers who wanted to rent out their places. More apartments attracted more renters, which incentivized others to put their homes online, which begat more renters, and soon the Airbnb flywheel was turning fast. As Airbnb puts it, "Guests attract hosts, and hosts attract guests."

Flywheel, network effects, virtuous circle—call it what you want, this dynamic is a major reason why many tech markets are "winner take all" or "winner take most." Unlike cola or beer, digital categories like search and social media tend to favor a single, dominant company. Such dominance is due to network effects. People are on Facebook because other people are on Facebook; who needs a second social network? People are used to Google, and it works. Why would they switch?

It's an axiom of any network that the value of a company owning one grows exponentially as its users grow. As great-business hunters, we don't need to understand the math underpinning this, but it's nevertheless instructive.

Network effects follow what's referred to as Metcalfe's law, which states that a network's value equals the number of its connections, squared. One fax machine, according to Metcalfe's law, is worth 1^2, or 1 unit of value, but a network composed of two fax machines is worth 2^2, or 4, while a network with four fax machines is worth 4^2, or 16. The same is true of home rental sites like Airbnb, social networks like Facebook, and anything else that connects people. Like each turn of the flywheel, each additional user compounds the power of the network.

The word "network" has been around since the 1530s, when writers used it to describe the interlocking patterns found in English embroidery. It was first used in the modern sense to describe the system of rivers and canals that began to connect industrializing Britain in the 1830s. Alexander Graham Bell created AT&T in 1885 to build and operate what would come to be known as a telephone network; later, with the invention of radio and television, the interconnected stations across the nation were rightly called networks.

These networks were impressive for their time—but digital networks make previous networks look tiny. All previous networks covered only a single nation at most; Facebook, WhatsApp, and Airbnb reach the entire world's population. Their value is therefore exponentially greater than any network previously created. Before it was broken up in 1984, AT&T's network encompassed 235 million Americans, but Facebook's network has nearly 3 billion regular monthly users. Facebook's network is thus more than a dozen times bigger than AT&T's was, and if we follow Metcalfe's law and further assume that the networks' users were of equal value, then Facebook's network is one hundred and fifty times more valuable than AT&T's network ever was.

Note: this exponentially higher value of digital networks is merely a theoretical construct. Like John Burr Williams's theory of discounted cash flow, we can't use Metcalfe's law to value digital companies. However, the law highlights the immense value of the new businesses born in the Digital Age.

Even Metcalfe's law doesn't fully capture the power of digital networks, because the calculation doesn't account for the fact that Facebook, Google, and similar businesses spent almost no money to build them out. Tech platforms are unique in history thanks to their global reach, but they are unique in another important respect: their networks run on infrastructure built and paid for by someone else.

Unlike Britain's early network of industrial waterways, tech software companies didn't have to spend billions to dig canals; tech hardware companies did that for them, competing against one another to make ever more powerful routers and long-haul internet connections. Unlike a telephone network, tech networks were not required to string wires and cables up and down mountains and over river gorges. Those wires already existed—and when they didn't, phone companies like AT&T and Verizon built expensive wireless networks to supplement them. Hardware companies like Cisco, Alcatel, and Lucent have made tremendous contributions to human progress by manufacturing the gear essential to such networks, but because these businesses produced commodities—wires, routers, and so on—their shareholders were never rewarded. Most of the value of the network we call the internet accrued to the software companies that made it easy to search, shop, chat, and perform other important functions online.

Never before have companies with such global reach spent so little to attain it. No wonder Buffett and Munger marvel at the economics of the Digital Age, and no wonder tech companies have become so big, so fast.

CHAPTER 6

Management: Some Things Never Change

I own both Alphabet and Amazon in client portfolios, but Alphabet has the better set of businesses. Software-based and requiring few assets to run, Alphabet is the perfect example of a Value 3.0 company. By contrast, both of Amazon's major businesses have distinct old-world characteristics. Amazon has spent billions building out a physical network for its e-commerce division, and it has done much the same for Amazon Web Services, its cloud computing subsidiary. All else being equal, Alphabet should be the better performer—but the chart opposite tells us otherwise.

What explains Amazon's outperformance? Management.

Both companies are hugely ambitious and unafraid to spend money, but Amazon's spending is much more targeted and financially sophisticated. While Alphabet funds dozens of speculative "moonshot" projects that lose billions of dollars a year, Amazon founder Jeff Bezos has kept his Blue Origin space venture outside the company; he pays for it with his own money. Amazon confronts problems with a rigorous, information-driven approach that resembles a good investor's. "Many of the important decisions we make at Amazon.com can be made with data," Bezos wrote in 2005. "There is a right answer or a wrong answer, a better answer or a worse answer, and math tells us which is which. These are our favorite kinds of decisions." You'll find little such clar-

Total return since Google's IPO in August of 2004

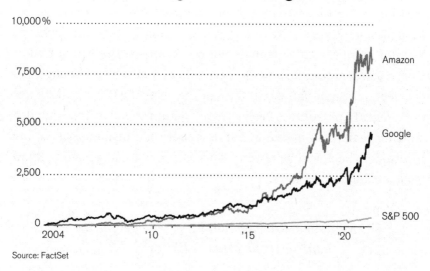

Source: FactSet

ity and precision in Alphabet's historical correspondence,* but every year, Bezos makes the following promise to his shareholders: "We will continue to measure our programs and the effectiveness of our investments analytically, to jettison those that do not provide acceptable returns, and to step up our investment in those that work best." The company's performance is directly correlated with such statements.

How can we identify managers who possess the same sort of long-term rigor and discipline that Bezos has exhibited? What are the markers that indicate a management team will work in your best interests as a shareholder? These are not easy questions to answer, but after studying the Mendelsons and HEICO, I was able to frame the management quality issue by posing two key questions:

1. Do the people in charge think and act like owners?
2. Do the managers understand what drives business value?

---

* Alphabet's lack of focus is beginning to change now that the company's founders have ceded operational control to a non-founder. As I explore in chapter 9, this management change is a major reason to be optimistic about Alphabet as an investment.

Unlike business quality and price, when it comes to management quality, we don't have to modify our approach for the Digital Age. Although many things have changed over the last generation, what to look for in an executive team is not one of them. The two questions I pose above would be equally pertinent if you were evaluating the overseer of a Sumerian wheat farm or the head of a Qing dynasty rice brokerage. To paraphrase Peter Lynch's dictum about business quality, superior management teams will do better than mediocre ones, and investors in each will be rewarded accordingly. We just need to know what attributes to look for.

Management Question #1: Do the people in charge think and act like owners?

Good managers treat the business they're running as if it's their own, even if it's not. If you're unacquainted with the ways of Wall Street, it may surprise you that most executives don't behave this way. To use Carl Icahn's colorful and accurate metaphor, most managers act as if they're caretakers of a vast English estate whose owners aren't paying much attention. Free to do as they please, the caretakers run the enterprise principally for their own enrichment rather than the owners'.

This behavior can be explained by the institutionalized nature of much of corporate America. To succeed at a big company, an executive must prove himself or herself for decades. A CEO usually becomes one at age fifty or older, and the average tenure of a Fortune 500 chief executive is roughly a decade. When they get to the top, with about ten years to get anything done, most top executives aren't interested in positioning the company for the long term. Rather, they're incentivized to keep the company on a steady course and out of trouble—and to get as personally rich as possible.

These are not the managers we want. We want the ones who put long-term stewardship ahead of self-interest. Later in the chapter, we'll explore specific traits you can look for to identify such executives.

Management Question #2: Do the managers understand what drives business value?

Every senior executive should obsess over his or her business, but such obsession isn't sufficient to make a manager great. What separates competent executives from excellent ones is a specific understanding of a few key metrics that correlate with long-term wealth creation. Managers should be familiar with the different types of competitive advantage that we covered in the previous chapter, but this understanding must be paired with the regular use of a few specific financial gauges. Such metrics will help them monitor how well they are translating their company's qualitative edge into quantitative, market-beating results.

Without this dashboard, no matter how obsessed they are with their business, corporate leaders are not going to deliver superior long-term results. Without an understanding of the basic equations that drive and determine business value, they will be like someone who wants to operate a railroad locomotive, is prepared to think and act like a locomotive operator, but who doesn't understand how the locomotive actually works.

Here again, you'd be surprised how common such ignorance is in the world of public companies. When I was at Davis Selected Advisors, a large mutual fund, I often posed a question to test the financial acumen of the CEOs who visited our offices. It involved return on capital, one of the key metrics every executive should understand and internalize.

"Which is more important for you to focus on: growth in sales and profits, or return on capital?" I would ask. As we'll explore later in the chapter, the answer is return on capital. Given enough capital to invest, anybody can grow sales and profits. It's the return on your investment that matters.

Roughly 80% of the CEOs got the answer wrong. One mumbled and bumbled for so long that it became obvious he didn't understand the question; embarrassed for him, I changed the subject. Another was more decisive but less correct. "Sales and profits," he answered without hesitation. The next day, however, he called me from his company's headquarters in Houston to tell me that he'd changed his mind. "Return on capital is more important," he said.

I was happy to hear that he'd arrived at the right answer, but unhappy to realize he'd most likely got the correct response from his chief financial officer, who is trained in such principles but often lacks the power to apply them.

During my time at Davis, I noticed that the CEOs most eager to visit our offices usually oversaw the most mediocre companies. Their skill set inclined more to schmoozing, so they must have figured that the best route to stock price outperformance was trying to persuade investors to buy their stock. This strategy never works. Market performance is driven over time by business performance, and business performance is driven by focusing on metrics that drive business value. Office visits to investors is not one of those metrics.

Because of this, it was hard to get managers who were focused on substance to visit us: they were too busy running their company. We got Paul Walsh, a blunt Englishman who transformed Diageo from a middling conglomerate into a beer and spirits powerhouse, only once. Rick Lenny, the first outsider to run Hershey in more than one hundred years, did visit our offices regularly, but when he did, he would come alone, without the usual minions. I began to use this metric as another informal management quality litmus test: how big an entourage the CEO turned up with was often inversely correlated with the stock price performance of that company. Carly Fiorina, the CEO of Hewlett-Packard, always had a large team in tow. Not only that, we knew about her visits weeks ahead of time, because her security detail sent a team of bomb-sniffing dogs well ahead of each one. It didn't surprise me when HP's stock price badly lagged the market average during Fiorina's tenure.

TOM MURPHY: THINKING AND ACTING LIKE AN OWNER

Often the best way to begin evaluating management teams is to evaluate the ones you know best: your own company's or those working in your own industry. Paying attention to executives you're familiar with is not illegal insider information. It's an integral part of Peter Lynch's "invest in what you know" strategy—except with management, it's not what you know, it's who you know. Information and insights that you pick up through your everyday experience are part of what securities lawyers call the mosaic theory of investing. Under this legal doctrine, investors collect tidbits of information here and there and use them over time to form an investment conclusion. Each data point is trivial by itself, but when you put them together they form a picture, just like individual mosaic tiles do when assembled.

You don't even need to work in a particular industry to find tiles that give you management clues. In a bit of deduction that should make it into the Commonsensical Investing Hall of Fame, a bartender who worked corporate functions in the 1970s bought stock in a company after observing how a particular executive team acted during a management retreat. What the bartender noticed was a relaxed and unpretentious culture with none of the sucking up usually evident at company parties. People seemed empowered rather than fearful, and that, the bartender deduced, was worth paying attention to. "I've worked a lot of corporate events over the years," he later explained, "but Capital Cities was the only company where you couldn't tell who the bosses were."*

We met Capital Cities in chapter 3. It's the local TV station operator that Buffett invested in heavily in 1985. Buffett bought so much Cap Cities stock for two reasons. The first had to do with business quality:

---

* This story, and many others, are told in *The Outsiders: Eight Unconventional CEOs and Their Radically Rational Blueprint for Success* by William N. Thorndike Jr. *The Outsiders* is the best book I've read on the qualities to look for when evaluating CEOs.

broadcasting was a great business in the latter part of the twentieth century, a toll bridge that advertisers had to cross to reach consumers. The second reason had to do with management quality: for thirty years, Cap Cities was run by Tom Murphy, a manager Buffett trusted so much that Buffett gave Murphy voting power over the Cap Cities' shares that Berkshire Hathaway owned.

"Most of what I learned about management," Buffett has said, "I learned from Murph." Perhaps we, too, can learn something.

———————

Why did Buffett trust and admire Murphy so much? To begin, he prized qualities in Murphy that most of us prize in others: honesty, humility, intelligence. He also appreciated the low-key, decentralized, "power-down" culture that the bartender observed. But what Buffett liked most about Murphy is that while he never owned more than 1% of the company, Murphy *acted* like an owner. Endowed with an old-world sense of stewardship, Murphy put the owners' interests first.

Such a mentality should top your list of management qualities to look for. Thankfully, it's so unusual that it's easily spotted. In Murphy's case, his devotion to the shareholders manifested itself in a frugality that bordered on the neurotic. When Murphy was running the Albany station WTEN, his boss ordered him to paint the outside of the company's run-down local headquarters. Murphy painted the two sides that faced the street; he left the other two sides, which faced a highway, untouched. Murphy's parsimony did not diminish after he became CEO of Cap Cities and then of the much larger Cap Cities–ABC combination. Prior to Cap Cities' takeover, ABC's New York executives went home at night in chauffeured limousines. When Murphy took over, they got around town in cabs, the same way Murphy did. When they had to go to Los Angeles, they flew like Murphy flew: in coach.

Murphy's story is instructive because although he was frugal, he was not miserly. When it came to important budget items, nobody in the broadcast business spent more than he did. This tendency is another important marker of excellent managers: *They target their spending for maximum effect.*

In Murphy's case, this meant leaving external walls unpainted while spending lavishly on the newsrooms inside those walls. Murphy asked himself: How can I drive the profitability of my TV stations higher? Cutting costs would do it, at least in the short term, but in the long run the local TV business was about attracting advertising dollars, and cutting the budget would impair Cap Cities' ability to attract them. A better method was to play offense. Murphy knew that whichever station dominated the evening news dominated the entire night, because viewers who tuned in for the 6:00 broadcast tended to stay on that channel until it was time to go to bed. The station that attracted the most viewers, Murphy reasoned, would also attract the most ad dollars from the local car dealers and grocery stores.

To dominate the local news, Murphy had to spend money to attract top newsroom talent and to build the best-looking sets. But he also knew that, once in place, this cost structure was fixed, while every incremental ad that Murphy managed to draw away from competitors would come in at a 100% profit margin.

Once he'd executed this strategy, it became clear that Murphy's reasoning had been correct. While Cap Cities' newsroom expenditures were the highest in the industry, so were its profit margins. The average local television station's operating margin was 25%, but Murphy's stations earned twice that.

UNDERSTANDING THE DRIVERS
OF SHAREHOLDER VALUE

As Cap Cities' margins show, Murphy understood how to build an outperforming company. Not only did Murphy grow Cap Cities into an industry giant, Cap Cities' stock price compounded at twice the rate of the market average during his tenure.

Ironically, however, learning how to build a successful financial engine begins with an indifference to the particulars of the locomotive itself. What separates competent managers from extraordinary ones is an abstract and mathematical understanding of value creation. Great managers don't care if they're in the television business or the widget business; they've subordinated any affection they feel for their business to a more general passion for making the owners wealthy. This kind of indifference allows managers to be clear-eyed when making decisions. In this way, great managers are like value investors: they remain disciplined in their investments. Like Larry Mendelson at HEICO, their principal business is the business of generating cash flow.

The best managers focus on a metric that captures both spending through the income statement and longer-term capital investments: return on capital. You don't have to know how to calculate return on capital, which can be measured in many ways. However, if you're serious about picking long-term investment winners, you should understand what return on capital looks like and why it matters.

NET OPERATING PROFIT AFTER TAX

÷ <u>INVESTED CAPITAL</u>

= RETURN ON CAPITAL

The numerator is simply how much a company is presently earning, disregarding interest costs. This is the "return" in the return on capital. The denominator, the "capital," is the amount of money the company has had to invest to generate the return.

Let's say we give our kids $25 to set up a corner lemonade stand over the weekend. The $25 represents their "capital," with which they buy lemons, sugar, paper cups, and so forth. Most parents are happy to let it go at that, but if they were financially inclined, they might ask their kids a series of questions on Sunday night when business was done. "We invested $25 in your lemonade stand: What was the return on that capital? Did you generate $1, $2.50, or $5 in profit?"

A $1 profit would have generated a 4% return on capital ($1/$25), which is poor; a $2.50 return would have given them a 10% return, which is average; but a $5 return equates to a 20% return on capital, which is superior. HEICO's return on capital is in this range.

If you engaged in this line of inquiry with your children, you could rightly be called an eccentric parent. However, you would also have shared a secret with them that only the best managers understand: the more profit you can earn from the least amount of assets over a sustained period is the key quantitative measure of a successful long-term business. "The goal," as Tom Murphy once said, "is not to have the longest train but to arrive at the station first using the least fuel."

Be aware, however, that high returns attract competition, so if the kids made $5 on Saturday, you might ask, "Did the neighbors' kids notice and set up a rival stand across the street on Sunday? Did they undercut you on price—and, if so, how did you counter that move? Was your brand so strong that customers didn't stray? Or did you need to raise more capital to invest in signage to advertise?"

Whether it involves a lemonade stand, a wind farm, or a dating app, the art of deciding how to spend a company's money in a way that maximizes returns is known as "capital allocation." Don't let this lifeless term put you off. It's essential that you find managers who know how to allocate capital well. Executives who can run their everyday business are common, but those who know how to deploy a company's resources are rare.

A crucial part of capital allocation is knowing whether, when, and how to engage in mergers and acquisitions, because buying companies involves large capital outlays. Murphy knew how to do this well. The broadcast industry consolidated when Murphy was running Cap Cities and ABC, but Murphy understood when to participate in the consolidation and when to refrain. Like a good investor, he often waited for Mr. Market to give him an opportunity to buy at distressed prices. Often, such opportunities arose during a recession, when the advertising market dipped and broadcasters' profits were temporarily depressed. And while Murphy bid on dozens of media properties, he never won an auction—because he was never the highest bidder.

Whether or not a manager is wasteful or careful with his own company's stock is another crucial litmus test you should use. Using stock to pay for a merger is often harmful to both return on capital and an individual shareholder's fractional ownership of the company. If I own five shares of a company with one hundred total shares, I own 5% of the company—but if the company issues another one hundred shares, my ownership shrinks to 2.5%. Murphy never used company stock to buy another company; he did his deals with borrowed money, and after the deal was done, Murphy used Cap Cities' cash flow to pay back the debt he'd incurred.

If Murphy couldn't find an attractive acquisition candidate, he would buy shares of the company he knew best: his own. Buying back shares is the opposite of issuing them: it shrinks the share count and increases shareholders' proportional ownership. It's also excellent for a company's return on capital, because when a company uses excess cash to buy back shares, it shrinks its capital base. Over thirty years, Murphy bought back nearly 50% of Cap Cities' stock in the open market, often buying it in the same way he bought other media properties—when Mr. Market priced them on sale.

Murphy also gave out few stock option grants, either to himself or to his fellow employees. He knew that every share grant diluted existing owners. How executives reward employees, not least of all themselves, with free grants of ownership is another wonderful test for a management team; it separates the skimmers from the stewards. Buffett has said that any company issuing more than 1% of its current outstanding shares every year in either options or restricted stock units is giving too much away. As usual, his logic is clear: if a company grows 10% a year and employees get 2% of the stock annually, they are in effect being gifted 20% of the growth. It's no surprise that, during his time at Cap Cities, Murphy's annual stock grants averaged in the 1% range.

Although I think Buffett's 1% rule is sound, I should note that it's harder to hold tech companies to this standard. It's not uncommon to find a tech company granting 3% to 5% of its shares to employees every year. That's a number that would make Buffett and Murphy blush—or curse.

While profligate, these grants should be seen in the context of how many tech companies began. Most started corporate life so cash-poor that the only currency they could offer was stock options. That tech companies are growing so much faster than the average American corporation is another mitigating factor.

Still, we should be on the lookout for outlandish grants in the tech sector. Elon Musk is an engineering genius, but I will likely never invest a dime in any of his companies. He and his board have shown they don't respect fellow shareholders. In 2018, Tesla's board approved giving Musk 20 million stock options to, in the board's words, "incentivize his continued leadership of Tesla over the long-term." Those options, worth $2.3 billion at the time, diluted existing shareholders by 12%, and the logic of the grant is ludicrous. Musk already owned nearly 40 million shares, or more than 20% of the company. What more incentive did he need to run Tesla well?

Thankfully, the courts have so far declined to block shareholder lawsuits against Tesla for both breach of fiduciary duty and what the lawyers delicately call "unjust enrichment."

JEFF BEZOS: APPLYING OLD-SCHOOL FINANCE TO THE DIGITAL WORLD

Tom Murphy's story is instructive and inspiring, but it's also yesterday's story. Television networks are never going to regain the economic and cultural hold they once had on the world. Their business is one of the many that's been displaced by the Digital Age.

Fortunately, Murphy's wisdom abides in a few managers who run Value 3.0 companies. The qualities they possess are identical to Murphy's: integrity, stewardship, and a savviness in how wealth gets created. To help you recognize these attributes in the digital economy, I'll use Jeff Bezos, founder of Amazon, as an illustration.

What distinguishes Bezos from most other tech entrepreneurs is his career path in early adulthood. Nearly all digital founders start their companies straight out of a university computer-science program, and their grasp of finance is often not strong. Bezos, on the other hand, began his professional life at a hedge fund. His time on Wall Street taught him important quantitative metrics like return on capital; it also taught him important qualitative and experiential ones like Mr. Market. A Buffett fan, Bezos started Amazon familiar with financial principles, but as someone who graduated with a degree in electrical engineering, he also understood the digisphere. By combining old-school financial truths with an understanding of modern online commerce, Bezos has become one of the world's richest human beings.

From his first days running Amazon, Bezos made it clear not only that he was prepared to think and act like an owner but also that he knew how to do so. His first letter to shareholders shows how, though only thirty-three years old, Bezos had already synthesized new-economy with old-economy principles. Like Buffett's 1951 analysis of GEICO in *The Commercial and Financial Chronicle*, it's a remarkable document, a sort of Declaration of Independence from both financial ignorance and short-term Wall Street thinking. Bezos considers the letter so important that he has reprinted it in all of Amazon's subsequent annual reports, and rightly so. In only 1,500 words, Bezos manages to check nearly every single box of management quality.

If you study the excerpts from this inaugural letter below and internalize the concepts in them, you'll be equipped to identify those rare tech executives who think in a similarly sophisticated manner.

- *Think and act like an owner.* "We know our success will be largely affected by our ability to attract and retain a motivated employee base, each of whom must think like, and therefore must actually be, an owner."
- *Be smart and targeted with your spending.* "We will work hard to spend wisely and maintain our lean culture. We understand the importance of continually reinforcing a cost-conscious culture, particularly in a business incurring net losses."

- *Understand the interplay between financial metrics like return on capital and more qualitative measurements like competitive advantage.* "We will balance our focus on growth with emphasis on long-term profitability and capital management. At this stage, we choose to prioritize growth because we believe that scale is central to achieving the potential of our business model."

- *Drive for first-mover advantage and scale, then use both to drive to higher returns on capital.* "The stronger our market leadership, the more powerful our economic model. Market leadership can translate directly to higher revenue, higher profitability . . . and correspondingly stronger returns on invested capital."

- *Invest for the long term.* "We will continue to make investment decisions in light of long-term market leadership considerations rather than short-term profitability considerations or short-term Wall Street reactions."

- *Judge yourself by long-term stock market success.* "We believe that a fundamental measure of our success will be the shareholder value we create over the *long term*. This value will be a direct result of our ability to extend and solidify our current market leadership position."

In subsequent letters, Bezos's rare combination of discipline and sophistication continues to shine through. "To our shareowners," he began the 2014 letter. "A dreamy business offering has at least four characteristics. Customers love it, it can grow to very large size, it has strong returns on capital, and it's durable in time—with the potential to endure for decades. When you find one of these, don't just swipe right, get married." Value 3.0, indeed! In 2020, he wrote: "Any business that doesn't create value for those it touches, even if it appears successful on the surface, isn't long for this world. It's on the way out."

Some complain that Bezos drives his employees too hard, and that may be true. On the other hand, he doesn't ask anything of them that he doesn't ask of himself. He is driven to create shareholder value, and he knows how to do it. Like Murphy, he compensates himself modestly; unlike Musk, Bezos has never taken a single stock option grant. Bezos must figure that the 10% of Amazon he owns, now worth roughly $170 billion, is enough to incentivize him. Equally impressive, Bezos manages to keep the number of options he grants to employees to a manageable 1% to 2% of total shares outstanding.

As for Bezos's annual pay, Amazon's latest proxy filing says that Bezos's compensation was $1.7 million—but that includes $1.6 million for a security detail. Bezos's actual cash earnings for 2020 was $81,480, an increase of only 3% from his starting pay twenty-five years ago. Meanwhile, during that time, Amazon's share price has grown 219,900%. Thus, while Bezos's salary has compounded at 0.1% annually, the Amazon shares he owns have compounded at 38% per year.

CHAPTER 7

Price and the Value 3.0 Toolbox

In 2021, Bezos kicked himself upstairs to become Amazon's chairman, but while he was CEO, like all financially savvy executives, he consulted a few simple gauges to keep track of how much shareholder value he was creating. Return on capital was on the dashboard, and so were profit margins, but Bezos would have shut down Amazon a long time ago if he had relied on the company's reported numbers. For nearly a third of Amazon's corporate history, its reported profits and returns on capital have been negative.

Like so many tech executives, Bezos had to adjust the financial statements to see what was going on in his business. If we are to capture the value that digital companies like Amazon are creating, we must do the same.

When it did turn a profit, Amazon never had any trouble reporting a good return on capital, because it built its massive distribution network largely on someone else's nickel. This is thanks to a phenomenon called "negative working capital," in which a company receives cash from its customers before it must pay its suppliers. Amazon's customers pay immediately, but Amazon uses its market power to delay paying the booksellers, the electronics manufacturers, and the rest. The result is a flywheel of more cash coming in than going out—negative working capital—and companies lucky enough to have it use it to fund their operations.

Even when it did turn a profit, however, Amazon has always been expensive when judged by its current price/earnings multiple. You can see this from the table below: it shows Amazon's mid-year stock price divided by its annual earnings from 1997 until 2020. Even though Amazon's stock has been on average nearly ten times more expensive than the market average, it has appreciated more than 2,300 times since its IPO. The market's total return is only eightfold.

This discrepancy raises two obvious questions:

- How has a stock that has been ten times more expensive than the overall market outperformed it by a factor of nearly 300?
- How can I, as a value investor, justify owning it despite its apparent priciness?

Expensive All the Way Up

Amazon P/E multiple vs. the market multiple

N/A = no earnings

	1997	'98	'99	2000	'01	'02	'03	'04
Amazon	N/A	N/A	N/A	N/A	N/A	N/A	214x	89x
S&P 500	22x	26x	30x	27x	23x	24x	20x	19x

	2005	'06	'07	'08	'09	'10	'11	'12
	36x	61x	152x	65x	60x	52x	81x	167x
	17x	16x	17x	19x	18x	14x	15x	14x

	2013	'14	'15	'16	'17	'18	'19	'20
	734x	529x	N/A	569x	197x	373x	94x	120x
	16x	18x	18x	20x	21x	20x	19x	24x

	AVERAGE
Amazon	211x
S&P 500	22x

Source: FactSet

The answers go a long way to solving the riddle of why value investing has failed to capture the value of tech. The answers also point us to specific ways we can refine value investing so that it becomes an effective tool in the digital world.

Price remains an essential component in a Value 3.0 framework. I don't propose that, like growth investors, we ignore price to focus only on the business's future. Nor do I think that we should "buy tech" as part of a momentum-based strategy simply because it continues to appreciate. To a value investor, there will always be prices so high that not even the best business is worth it. You may fall in love with a Fifth Avenue penthouse when you see its many rooms and its Central Park views, but you'd be wise to walk away if the broker asks $5 billion for it.

However, it's also important to acknowledge that, as value investors, today we lack the numerical vocabulary required to articulate how the Digital Age is creating such wealth. It's not just Amazon that has beaten the market despite looking expensive on value metrics. Hundreds of tech companies, large and small, have outperformed despite reporting little to no earnings. Value investing must reckon with this fact, and with the fact that value investing doesn't yet possess the tools required to analyze such companies. Once we acknowledge this reality, we can go through the value toolbox and decide which instruments still work, which ones don't, and which ones need to be modified.

VALUATION TOOLS TO SET ASIDE

Price to book and other asset-based metrics. When Buffett shifted his lens to focus not on what a company owned but what it earned, he rejected his mentor's framework and moved value investing from Value 1.0 to Value 2.0. Since then, the economy has become even less dependent on hard, tangible assets, and Ben Graham's asset-based approach has become even less useful.

You'd be surprised, however, how many value investors cling to this old, asset-based discipline. I recently read a research report urging me to buy Adient, the world's largest manufacturer of automobile seats, because it was cheap based on the factories and inventories it owned. The report's author wanted me to ignore the fact that Adient operates in a mature, commoditized, and competitive industry; that its net profit margins are in the low single digits; and that, over the last several years, its return on capital has been subpar. In today's asset-light economy, to even consider investing in such an old, beaten-down business seems masochistic.

Putting aside Graham's asset-based approach has a secondary benefit as well: it allows us to separate Graham's lasting contributions from his transient ones. Ben Graham's real legacy is not that he gave us a specific discipline; it's that he introduced investors to *the idea of discipline itself.*

The importance of discipline and rigor remains constant, but its specifics should remain fluid and flexible. They should change as the world changes. Capital-intensive factories once drove most of the world's economic value, but that's no longer true. Software drives today's economy, and because software requires few assets to generate large income streams, physical assets have become largely irrelevant.*

It would be wrong to say, however, that we should discard asset-based metrics for good. During times of extreme market stress, companies occasionally sell at attractive prices relative to their asset values. In the dot-com bust, I bought Apple for the liquidation value of its cash and Silicon Valley real estate. In 2009, the market was so panicked that I was able to buy Movado, a solid mid-market watch brand, for less than the value of its current assets minus its entire liabilities. Thanks to the financial crisis, I found the rarest of species in today's ecosystem: a classic Graham "net net."

Thus, while we shouldn't use asset valuation in our normal work, we should stow this tool away and bring it out only when Mr. Market is in a deep funk.

---

* Entire books have been written about this subject, including *Capitalism Without Capital: The Rise of the Intangible Economy* by Jonathan Haskel and Stian Westlake, which I recommend.

Reversion to the mean. When nothing much changes in the economic landscape, "this time it's different" are dangerous words for an investor. During such times, sectors go in and out of favor but eventually return to normal, so the trick to beating the market is to rotate among them.

Sometime in the early twenty-first century, however, the Digital Age gained critical mass, and "this time it's different" became an accurate rather than a dangerous statement. Tech has disrupted the normal ebb and flow of so many once-reliable industries that it sometimes feels as if most of the legacy economy is under attack. According to calculations by T. Rowe Price portfolio manager David Giroux, at least one-third of the non–tech market capitalization of the S&P 500 is now at risk of being disrupted by technological change. I think the figure could be closer to 50%.

In such a rapidly changing world, how is betting that things will go back to normal a sensible strategy? How are legacy industries like brick-and-mortar retailers and TV broadcasters somehow going to "return to normal"? Conversely, what is "normal" for tech companies armed with competitive advantages and single-digit shares of their addressable markets? Isn't it more analytically accurate to say that, instead of oscillating around some historical mean, many tech companies are just now achieving escape velocity?

TOOLS TO KEEP BUT MODIFY

Like Buffett's Value 2.0, Value 3.0 uses cash earnings as its valuation north star. What John Burr Williams wrote in *The Theory of Investment Value* more than eighty years ago remains true: the value of any business is the sum of all its future free cash flows, discounted back to the present at an appropriate interest rate. As a practical matter, however, it's impossible and therefore fruitless to forecast such cash flows beyond a few years. The future is unpredictable and, outside a certain time horizon, completely unknowable. That's why the price/earnings ratio based on current earnings has become such a popular shorthand:

I'm paying $X for $Y in earnings that I can see today. Everything else is unclear.

What is clear, however, is that the P/E ratio based on current earnings has not captured the value that tech has created. If it had, Value 2.0 investors would have done exceedingly well with Amazon, Alphabet, and the rest over the last two decades. Instead, most value managers have underperformed the market rather badly, sniffing all the way at tech stocks as "expensive." Because we've not adapted our methods, we've missed out on nearly a generation of wealth creation.

After my own period of underperformance in the mid-2010s, I broke the P/E tool down, trying to figure out why it wasn't working and how I could modify it so that it would work again. In the end, I have altered the P/E construct in two material ways.

First, instead of looking only at this year's or next year's earnings, I look at earnings several years out. This exercise is not based on some wild-eyed dream of "the future." I don't propose to project out a decade, or even five years: nobody knows what's going to happen that far out. On the other hand, certain digital companies have such strong competitive moats and are so early in their growth trajectory that it's reasonable to forecast what their business will look like in a few years. What is the likelihood that Alphabet will grow its business over the next thirty-six months? What is the likelihood that Airbnb, DocuSign, Adobe, and dozens of other digital enterprises will continue to penetrate their markets? I think most reasonable people would agree that it's probable such companies will grow over the next few years.

The second adjustment I make is more radical and more dramatic. It involves the concept of earnings power, which I introduced in chapter 4 when I compared Campbell's to Intuit. While Campbell's business is mature and therefore in harvest mode, Intuit's is not. Faced with slow growth, Campbell's is rightfully milking its business for every dollar of current earnings that it can. Intuit, on the other hand, is deploying billions into sales and marketing and research and development to grow future earnings. This spending is anchored in sound business logic, but it has the effect of depressing Intuit's current reported profits.

Such aggressive spending behavior is common among tech companies. Facebook, Alphabet, Amazon, Apple, and Microsoft alone recorded a combined $125 billion in R & D in 2020, a figure that's larger than any state budget in the Union except for New York and California. As a result, the profits of many tech companies resemble Intuit's: they are artificially depressed. Walmart's reported margins are triple that of Amazon's e-commerce margins, for example—does anyone believe that a brick-and-mortar retailer is inherently three times more profitable than a digital one? Is it plausible that Walmart, which must maintain thousands of physical stores and pay millions of employees to staff them, could earn three times as much on every sales dollar as a retailer doing business online? If you choose to focus on Amazon's reported earnings, this is what you are implicitly assenting to.

As the Digital Age unfolds, it's increasingly obvious that a tech company's current income statement is an unreliable measure of its long-term ability to generate free cash flow. The P/E multiple remains a good shorthand tool to get at a company's value, we need to adjust a digital company's income statement to arrive at its earnings power. Earnings power seeks to capture the underlying potential of what companies like Intuit and Amazon could earn if they weren't investing billions to grow their markets.

Many have mocked such spending as reckless and rashly conceived, but two decades of experience have proven that tech executives were right to make such investments. Tech's massive spending isn't foolish or crazy; it is rational. Tech executives are the most data-driven in history. They are spending money because they believe that, in aggregate, their investments will deliver an eventual good return on capital. Investors, however, can't see such returns because of today's outdated accounting conventions. These rules, promulgated as generally accepted accounting principles, or GAAP, must be seen in their historical context.

After the Crash of 1929 and the Great Depression, the government created the Securities and Exchange Commission, which was given the mandate to set accounting standards. The SEC delegated this responsibility to the accounting profession, which has promulgated several versions of standard practices, the latest of which is GAAP.

While GAAP undergoes constant modification, its roots lie in the Industrial Age, and it has been slow to adapt to the digital realities of the early twenty-first-century economy. Like an older investor, it's more comfortable with old-economy companies than new ones. As a result, it rewards old-economy investments like factories and penalizes new-economy spending on items like research and development.

Specifically, GAAP requires nearly 100% of R & D and marketing outlays to be immediately expensed, while it allows hard assets like property, plant, and equipment to be depreciated over many years. To depreciate means to amortize, or slowly kill; so when a company depreciates an asset, it recognizes the expense only gradually. Old-economy assets like factories are considered long-term investments, and expenditures on them can be recognized through the income statement over 20 to 30 years. Tech companies, however, have little need for factories. Their biggest investments are in developing and marketing their products—but according to GAAP, most of these expenses must be recognized immediately.

Such differences in accounting treatment lead to startling differences between the income statement of an old-economy company and the income statement of a digital company. An industrial business that invests $100 million in a plant with an estimated twenty-five-year life recognizes only $4 million a year in expense for that plant. By contrast, a tech company that spends $100 million on consumer-focused research and development must recognize that entire $100 million as expense right away. If both companies had revenues of $100 million and no other expenses, the industrial company's profits would be $96 million. As the following chart shows, the tech company's profits would be zero.

This is a nonsensical result, but according to GAAP, it's the correct one. Today's accounting rules make old-economy income statements

Different accounting = Different results

	Industrial company	Tech company
Revenues	$100,000,000	$100,000,000
Expense	$4,000,000	$100,000,000
Operating income	$96,000,000	–

look unreasonably attractive and new-economy ones look unreasonably ugly.

The distortions are so great that various parts of the business community have suggested remedies to bring accounting more in line with economic reality. A generation ago, consultant Bennett Stewart introduced the world to the principle of economic value added, or EVA, which recasts financial statements by expensing most R & D over five years and most marketing over three years. EVA's tools allow investors to adjust income statements on their own, but some accountants think it's time to overhaul GAAP entirely so that it can properly measure profit and loss in the Digital Age. Two professors, Baruch Lev and Feng Gu, have written a provocative book on the topic with an equally provocative title: *The End of Accounting.*

I don't claim to know whether the proper life of an R & D expenditure is three years, five years, or ten years. Figuring that out is a tricky exercise, and one that I will leave to those who oversee GAAP. I do know, however, that a one-year life for many R & D expenditures in today's economy is just wrong. Historically, R & D has been expensed immediately because such spending was rightly regarded as speculative— but the world has changed. Tech's spending today is much less "R," or pure research, and much more "D," or development. Development is far from speculative; it is by definition the implementation of ideas that have already been tested. Does every dollar that Alphabet deploys to improve its search engine generate only a 365-day return? When Microsoft spends money to refine its suite of Office tools, do the benefits last only one year? Such assertions are, as the lawyers like to say, absurd on their face—and yet that is how such expenditures are accounted for today.

As a result, digital businesses wisely ignore GAAP and instead recast their financial statements for internal use. Many use a metric called "LTV to CAC," which sounds complicated but is really just a workaround to convert marketing expenditures into marketing investments. Instead of running marketing spending through the income statement, companies such as Intuit convert it to a capital outlay so that the company can measure its effectiveness. For every $1 spent to acquire a new customer (customer acquisition cost, or "CAC"), Intuit wants to generate $3 in lifetime revenue from that customer (lifetime value, or "LTV"). Assuming it hits that bogie, and assuming a 20% net margin, Intuit will generate sixty cents on every $1 of investment, for a 60% return on capital.

That's an excellent return—except this return is not apparent from Intuit's financial statements. All of Intuit's marketing dollars are expensed rather than capitalized and depreciated.

LTV/CAC sounds like a newfangled metric, and I can hear old-school value investors griping, "How can you know what the lifetime value of a customer is?" Making such estimates and adjustments, however, is not magical thinking; it's *rational* thinking. Analysts from Graham to Bezos to Buffett have reconfigured financial statements when economic reality required it.

One of the best examples of this involves GEICO, the security Buffett liked best in 1951. Buffett bought GEICO shares in the public market throughout his career, and by 1995 Berkshire Hathaway owned 51% of the company. That year he bought the rest, making GEICO one of Berkshire's many wholly owned subsidiaries.

In the final year that GEICO was a public company, it earned $250 million in net income while spending $33 million on advertising and marketing, every dollar of which was expensed per GAAP's rules. Four years later, as a Berkshire subsidiary, GEICO reported that it had increased marketing spending to nearly $250 million, a figure equal to GEICO's entire earnings of just a few years before. Did that mean that

GEICO was now earning zero? Or did it mean that Buffett was *deliberately tanking current earnings because he knew that GEICO's marketing spend would generate more profits in the future*?

Of course, the latter is true. Buffett had identified GEICO as one of the few businesses in the pre–Digital Age that had both a competitive advantage and exponential growth opportunities. He thus proceeded in the same fashion that tech companies are proceeding now: he put economic reality ahead of accounting convention and invested heavily in the future. Buffett understood that if he could spend marketing dollars today to add profitable customers for years, it didn't matter if that depressed current earnings. He said as much in his 1999 annual shareholder letter. "Though GEICO's intrinsic value should grow by a highly satisfying amount," he wrote, "its [profit] performance is almost certain to weaken. That's . . . because we will materially increase our marketing expenditures."

Damn the accounting rules, Buffett was saying, I'm going to make the investment because it makes economic sense. Even though it depressed current earnings, Buffett believed the increased spending would make GEICO more valuable in the future. How is his decision a generation ago any different from the ones that tech executives from Adobe to Zoom are making today?

CHAPTER 8

Earnings Power

I have bought and sold Amazon a half dozen times over my career, always buying it because the business and the management were good, and always selling it because the price seemed so expensive. It's obvious now that the former instinct was correct, while the latter was not. It wasn't until I combined the idea of business quality with the concept of earnings power that I felt comfortable owning Amazon for the long term.

In early 2020, the coronavirus crisis depressed Amazon's stock price by nearly 25%, but Amazon appeared, as usual, expensive. The market was asking me to pay roughly $2,000 per share for Amazon; meanwhile, the company had just reported $23 per share in GAAP net profit for 2019. Amazon was therefore selling for nearly ninety times earnings, which made Amazon five times more expensive on a P/E basis than the average publicly traded company.

Armed with my new earnings power tool, I decided to adjust Amazon's reported numbers to see what its underlying earnings potential might be. I knew that Amazon was spending much more on the future than the average company. I knew that accounting rules were penalizing Amazon for cash outlays that should be considered long-term investments. As a result, I knew that Amazon's earnings power would likely be materially higher than the $23 per share it reported—but how much higher? As a value investor, I needed to quantify rather than guess.

The resulting exercise involved two steps, neither of which involved any complicated math. Nor did it depend on arcane information. Nearly all the data I needed to begin, in fact, came from pages 67 and 68 of Amazon's 2019 annual SEC filing.

First, I projected the company's sales three years out into the future. Second, I recast reported earnings into a reasonable estimate of Amazon's earnings power. In doing so, I didn't overhaul the accounting rules, and I didn't use Bennett Stewart's EVA framework. I merely tried to use my common sense. I asked myself, what kind of profitability would Amazon report if it were a mature company in harvest mode? Often, I had publicly traded companies in similarly situated businesses to help me triangulate between my own conjecture and economic reality.

While not complex, the changes made it clear that Amazon passed not only the business quality and the management test, but the price one as well. Optically expensive at nearly ninety times current earnings, Amazon, I concluded, was trading for roughly fifteen times its earnings power. This multiple was not only well under my BMP hurdle for price; it made Amazon cheaper than the average American stock.

STEP #1: ROLL AMAZON'S REVENUES THREE YEARS FORWARD

When I forecast Amazon's 2019 revenues three years into the future, I could hear the old-school value analyst in me asking, "How can you project what you can't see?" All value investors are trained to believe that a bird in the hand is worth at least two in the bush. When I contemplated Amazon's two major businesses, however, it didn't seem aggressive to project their growth several years out. It seemed analytically correct.

In fact, it seemed that it would be irrational *not* to project any sales growth. If Amazon had been a mature business, or if its competitive footing were shaky, I would have had no grounds to make such assumptions. But shopping online is a demonstrably easier and cheaper way to shop, and Amazon is the clear leader in e-commerce. Even after substantial growth, "e-tail" still represents only a small part of total retail sales. How is Amazon not going to grow? The dynamics were similar for cloud computing, Amazon's other major business.

To be conservative, I decelerated the five-year historical growth rate of cloud computing, Amazon's fastest-growing segment, from 35% to 30%. I kept e-commerce's historical 20% growth rate constant because I thought it was more sustainable. I felt this assumption was conservative, given that the pandemic was accelerating the move to online commerce.*

STEP #2: ADJUST AMAZON'S MARGINS TO REFLECT ECONOMIC REALITY

Like Berkshire Hathaway, Amazon is a conglomerate that owns many different businesses. Under its roof, you can find e-commerce, subscription services like Prime and Amazon Music, hardware devices like Alexa and Kindle, cloud computing, and Whole Foods grocery stores. To make it easier for investors to understand all these businesses, Amazon consolidates them into six major reporting segments. Here they are as I found them in the company's 2019 SEC filing:

Amazon's net sales by business segment, in millions

	2017	2018	2019
Online stores	$108,354	$122,987	$141,247
Physical stores	5,798	17,224	17,192
Third-party seller services	31,881	42,745	53,762
Subscription services	9,721	14,168	19,210
Other	4,653	10,108	14,085
Cloud division	17,459	25,655	35,026
Total sales	**$177,866**	**$232,887**	**$280,522**

Source: company SEC filings

---

* With two years of hindsight, I was indeed conservative, at least as far as 2020 was concerned. Cloud computing grew at 30%, right in line with my three-year projection. E-commerce, however, was turbocharged by stay-at-home pandemic shopping and grew by nearly 40%, double my annualized growth projection. In only one year, Amazon's e-commerce segment was already more than halfway to my projected revenues three years out.

Note that Amazon's presentation extends only to revenues; the company is much less forthcoming in disclosing details of operating income. Of its six segments, Amazon discloses the profits only of Amazon Web Services, its cloud division: $9.2 billion. On revenues of $35 billion, this equals a 25% operating margin. That's a healthy profit, and one consistent with other tech hardware companies that, like Amazon's cloud division, require lots of capital investment. It thus appeared to me that AWS was already operating at scale, and I didn't need to make any adjustments to arrive at a reasonable approximation of its earnings power.

As you can see in the graphic below, cloud computing represented most of Amazon's total $14.5 billion in reported operating profit. If the cloud division generated $9.2 billion and the entire company made $14.5 billion, it followed that Amazon's core e-commerce segment made $5.3 billion. On a sales denominator of $245 billion, this meant that the e-commerce's operating margins were only 2%.

This was the first of many figures in Amazon's financial statements that looked wrong. Grocery stores, a notoriously cutthroat, low-margin business, generate a 2% profit margin. Walmart generates 6%. Could Amazon, the world's leader in e-commerce, be only as profitable as a grocery store?

Amazon 2019 revenue and profit breakdown

As the math below shows, to believe Amazon's reported financial statements is to assent to e-commerce margins of 2%. Walmart's operating margins are 6%. Does anyone seriously believe that the world's leading e-commerce company is inherently $1/3$ as profitable as the world's leading brick and mortar retailer?

	Cloud division	Total company	Implied e-commerce
Revenue, in billions	$35.0	$280.5	$245.5
Operating income, in billions	$9.2	$14.5	$5.3
Operating margin	26%	5%	2%

Source: company SEC filings

I doubted it. For one thing, since its IPO Amazon has consistently said that the operating margins of its online retail business should at maturity be 10% to 13%.* For another, Walmart has more than 10,000 stores to maintain; Amazon has only 500 Whole Foods stores, a handful of Amazon branded stores, and fewer than 1,000 distribution centers. How could Walmart be three times more profitable than a company operating with less than 10% of a physical presence?

Here, I was confronted with one of those binary questions that are often very easy to resolve. Either there was something structurally broken with Amazon's online model, or the company was underreporting its true earnings power. It was clear to me, both from instinct and by making comparisons to comparable companies, that the latter was true. Other, less ambitious e-tailers such as eBay report 25% operating margins.

At this point, I could have just slapped Amazon's 10% to 13% long-term profitability goal on the entire e-commerce segment, or I could have imputed eBay's 25% margin to Amazon. Instead, I decided to dig another layer deeper. The company had given me discrete revenue—but not profit—disclosure for five of its commerce divisions. If I worked through the numbers of these subsidiaries and tried to tease out a profitability profile for each one, perhaps I could generate a more accurate estimate of Amazon's earnings power. So that's what I did.

1. *Online retail.* This is Amazon's largest and oldest segment, the legacy business that dates to Amazon's early bookselling days. In 2019, online retail accounted for half of all corporate revenues, so getting the margins right here was important.

Common sense told me that this segment's margins should be at least equal to Walmart's 6%. Several calculations seemed to back that up. Walmart's depreciation expense, the proxy for how much it must

---

* See for example Amazon's 2000 annual report: "Over the longer term, it is our objective that pro forma operating profit will reach the low double-digits as a percentage of net sales and our return on invested capital may reach the low triple-digits."

spend to maintain its physical plant, amounts to 2% of its annual sales. Amazon has no physical customer traffic in its virtual store, so it was logical to assume that Amazon's depreciation expense is de minimis by comparison. Moreover, because it operates online, Amazon does not have to worry about "shrink," the euphemism retailers use for shoplifting. While Walmart works hard to minimize theft—those "greeters" aren't at the door just to welcome you—last year Walmart lost roughly $5 billion to sticky fingers. This amounts to one percentage point of margin lost to shrink.

If we assume that Amazon's margins begin at Walmart's 6%, and then we add two points of depreciation that Amazon doesn't have to incur and one percentage point for shrink, Amazon's online retail earnings power becomes 9% of sales. That's half again as profitable as Walmart and roughly in line with Amazon's low double-digit goal.

In the end, I assigned a 10% operating margin to Amazon's legacy online store. Ten percent is just above the 9% margin I had calculated and at the low end of Amazon's long-term 10% to 13% aspiration.

Putting a 10% margin on $140 billion of core e-commerce sales generates $14 billion in earnings power. That is an interesting figure: it nearly equals Amazon's entire 2019 reported operating profit.

2. and **3.** *Physical stores and subscriptions.* When I looked at two of Amazon's smaller segments, physical stores and subscriptions, it was clear there would be no such dramatic changes. "Physical stores" refers mainly to Whole Foods Markets, which Amazon bought in 2017. Before its acquisition, Whole Foods was reporting operating margins in the 5% range, higher than the average grocer and consistent with Whole Foods' premium brand. Because this segment was less than 10% of Amazon's total corporate sales, however, it didn't matter whether I assigned physical stores a 2% margin, a 5% margin, or a 15% margin. The difference wouldn't have been big enough to affect Amazon's earnings power in a major way.

(This brings up an important point: When you're analyzing companies, make sure that the segment you're enthused about passes what accountants call the "materiality standard." If you were interested in Whole Foods as a driver of Amazon's value, running the numbers above would have persuaded you that it wasn't big enough to make a difference. You should be on the lookout for such traps. You may prefer Google's shopping platform to Amazon's, but that's not what drives Alphabet's value: search does.)

Like other major tech platforms, Amazon views its various subscriptions businesses not as profit centers but as ways to bind customers to its platform. To use the old grocery term, they run subscriptions as loss leaders, low-margin products that they know will draw people into their stores—and keep them coming back. Paying $139 a year for Amazon Prime delivery strikes many people as a good deal, but getting a free video service thrown in makes it even better. Amazon spends billions each year to populate its streaming service with compelling new shows. Because the company charges nothing for it, some might consider this spending wasteful. Amazon, however, views it as a good investment. Offering subscriptions is an attempt to build a "switching cost" moat. Having Prime Video makes customers less likely to drop their annual subscription for e-commerce delivery, where the company does make money.

Given all these puts and takes, it was hard for me to know how profitable Amazon's subscription segment was. On the one hand, Prime delivery brings in billions of annual revenues. On the other hand, free shipping costs Amazon a lot, and much of Prime's revenue goes straight to buying video content. Alibaba, one of the few tech platforms that reports operating profits in its subscriptions segment, runs this business at a loss. On the other hand, it doesn't have customers paying it $139 a year for delivery. Given this, I thought it was fair to assume that Amazon's subscriptions business ran at roughly breakeven, so I assigned this segment margins of zero.

4. *Third-party seller services.* When Amazon began online, it bought and sold merchandise the old-fashioned way: it purchased a book from a publisher, or a CD player from a manufacturer, then marked the product up and sold it for a profit. Gradually, however, Amazon opened its website to other merchants who lacked their own online presence, and this service proved enormously popular. In 2000, such third-party seller services represented only 3% of Amazon's gross merchandise sales, but by 2015 the figure surpassed 50%. Today, roughly two-thirds of all sales on the company's platform come from outside merchants.

These third-party sellers pay for the goods they sell on Amazon, and this arrangement has material implications for Amazon's profitability. When Amazon sells protein bars or a selfie stick on its website, but a third-party merchant pays for the goods, Amazon avoids the single biggest expense of a retailer: buying the merchandise itself. Moreover, Amazon charges these merchants a fee for the right to transact business on its platform. Because Amazon dominates e-commerce, merchants are happy to—or are forced to—pay for access to Amazon's eyeballs.

By turning its storefront into a place where the goods are paid for mainly by other merchants, Amazon has become a platform company. Like the fees Apple charges app developers, Amazon's third-party merchant fees have almost no expenses associated with them.

As a result, like Apple, Amazon has transformed itself from a relatively low-margin "hardware" business into one that can generate levels of profitability usually associated with software companies like Facebook and Alphabet. To use Buffett's metaphor, Amazon has become a toll bridge, and in 2019 it collected $54 billion in tolls from third-party merchants.

What are the margins associated with this revenue stream? Amazon discloses nothing about it, but I figured the margins had to be higher than traditional e-commerce. Amazon doesn't pay for the goods themselves, and the fees it charges merchants are pure gravy. However, Amazon stores, packs, and ships most third-party orders, and that costs a lot of money.

eBay is a pure third-party reseller and, as I mentioned earlier, enjoys operating margins of 25%. Was 25% the right profitability figure to assign this segment? On the one hand, eBay has almost no logistics operations. It leaves the shipping to its third-party merchants, and this fact suggests that margins for Amazon's third-party segment might be lower than 25%. On the other hand, eBay's single biggest expense is sales and marketing. Without Amazon's market power and instant brand recognition, eBay must spend 25 cents of every revenue dollar it earns to promote itself. Amazon has no such need.

In the end, I decided to give Amazon's third-party business segment the same 25% operating margins as eBay. eBay's higher marketing costs, I estimated, were roughly equivalent to Amazon's higher distribution costs. This estimate was nothing more than a guess, but it struck me as a sound one. If Amazon's legacy e-commerce margins were 10%, its third-party business was likely two to three times more profitable.

Assigning a 25% operating margin to Amazon's third-party revenues of $54 billion generated roughly $14 billion in operating profit. This is another interesting number: by assigning reasonable margins to both Amazon's traditional online segment and its third-party selling segment, I found that Amazon's earnings power was *roughly double* the company's entire reported operating profit. And I hadn't yet analyzed the company's most profitable segment: advertising.

5. *"Other"—i.e., advertising sales.* Amazon has turned its ubiquitous web presence into another powerful toll bridge. With the company averaging 90 million online visits per day, its website is becoming an increasingly popular place for companies to advertise. Amazon reports ads in its "other" segment, and in 2019 this segment generated $14 billion of revenue. According to a footnote on page 68 of the company's 2019 SEC filing, most of this revenue comes from selling ads.

This business is surely even more profitable than Amazon's third-party selling service. When selling goods for others, Amazon must still pay for the extra labor and the incremental distribution space associated with the merchandise. Advertising, on the other hand, takes place in the virtual world. Beyond perhaps paying a team of engineers to configure the ads, it doesn't cost Amazon anything at all.

What is the margin on this business? It likely approaches 100%. If, for argument's sake, we say that Amazon incurred $1 billion in annual engineering costs to run the ad segment, that would equate to a 93% profit margin. On the other hand, perhaps some of this "other revenue" was very low-margin. I doubted it—but to be conservative, I assigned this segment a 50% profit margin. This estimate added another $7 billion to Amazon's earnings power.

—————

What were the net results of my earnings power exercise? As you can see from the table that follows, Amazon's reported e-commerce profits were $5.3 billion—but its earnings power was $35 billion, or nearly seven times more.

When combined with projecting Amazon's revenues three years into the future, this adjustment had dramatic implications for the price the market was asking me to pay. The multiple on reported 2019 earnings was eighty-seven times, but the multiple on 2022's estimated earnings power was fifteen times. That moved the earnings yield from 1% to 7%.

—————

If, having worked through this exercise, you find the uncertainty in both financial statements and valuation unsettling, then I've done my job. As an investor, you must get used to a certain degree of haziness. The world is uncertain, the future is uncertain, and what counts as earnings is uncertain.

This lack of exactitude drives engineers like my son crazy. Engineers live by precision, and rightly so. A single line of bad code corrupts an entire program, and a millimeter off in the placement of a jet engine's fuel nozzle means the plane will malfunction. As anyone familiar with them knows, however, income statements and balance sheets are filled with all sorts of estimates.

Treating financial statements as gospel is especially dangerous in the Digital Age, because GAAP's old-economy bias distorts them so badly. The truth, however, is that beneath their neat, well-ruled sur-

Amazon's e-commerce *reported* earnings, 2019

E-commerce	Revenue	Operating margin	Operating income
	In billions		In billions
Online retail	$141	*Not reported*	–
Physical stores (Whole Foods)	$17	*Not reported*	–
Subscriptions	$19	*Not reported*	–
Third-party retail	$54	*Not reported*	–
Advertising	$14	*Not reported*	–
Total retail	**$245**	**2%**	**$5.3**

Amazon's corporate *reported* earnings, 2019

	Revenue	Operating margin	Operating income
	In billions, except per share data		
E-commerce	**$245**	**2%**	**$5.3**
Cloud division	$35	26%	$9.2
Total	**$280**	**5%**	**$14.5**

Earnings per share		**$23.01**
March 2020 stock price		$2,000
P/E multiple		**87x**

Source: Analysis of company SEC filings

Earnings power, 2019

Reasonable operating margin	Operating income In billions
10%	$14
2%	$0.3
0%	–
25%	$14
50%	$7
14%	**$35**

Earnings power, 2022

Estimated 2022 revenue In billions	Estimated operating margin	Operating income In billions
$423	**14%**	**$60**
$77	26%	$20
$500	**16%**	**$80**
		$132
		$2,000
		15x

face, a company's financial statements have always been somewhat squishy. Bad debt reserves, warranty expense, depreciation expense— all of these are not precise calculations. They are approximations that companies must make, and this leaves considerable room for fudging. "By making excessive or insufficient allowances for these items," Ben Graham wrote in 1937 about the depreciation reserve, "the net earnings may readily be under- or over-stated."

To get comfortable with such uncertainty, we can once again turn to Buffett as our role model. He has mastered it. It's good to be "directionally accurate," he frequently says, and also, quoting earlier investors, "it's better to be approximately right rather than precisely wrong." Though more intimate with financial statements than perhaps anyone else in the world, Buffett knows how easy it can be to get lost in the numbers and forget what really matters: moats or the lack thereof.

For this reason, Buffett calls himself a business analyst rather a financial or securities analyst. The difference, while subtle, is enormous. A financial analyst believes that the numbers drive performance, but a business analyst knows that the numbers, the ratios, and the stock's performance all derive from one thing: business quality.

Thus, while it's important to be reasonably accurate when determining earnings power, we should keep the exercise in perspective. What really matters is finding superior businesses that possess durable competitive advantages. Once we've done that, we can then make reasonable approximations of their earning power. Moreover, we should remember that earnings power isn't meant to be calculated down to the fourth decimal place. Used properly, earnings power can be a valuable tool, but it shouldn't be an exercise in precision.

We can see how earnings power be powerful while still being only "directionally accurate" by playing with some of the estimates I made to determine Amazon's earnings power. Let's say that you think my estimate of Amazon's online segment margins of 10% are too high. Fine— adjust them downward, to 5%, making them lower than Walmart's. This represents a major change in assumptions, but the net effect on valuation is trivial. The adjustment pushes the company's earnings power down 15%, and it raises the multiple from fifteen times to eighteen times. Let's say, on the other hand, you think my estimates of Amazon's margins are too low. You've used Bennett Stewart's EVA framework, expensing Amazon's sales and marketing costs over three years and its R & D over five, and you've calculated that Amazon's earnings-power multiple is twelve times. Again, it doesn't matter much to valuation. Whether the multiple is twelve times or eighteen times, Amazon is a table-pounding buy.

CHAPTER 9

BMP Case Studies: Alphabet and Intuit

We've run through each part of the BMP template—the quality of the business, the quality of the management, and the price the market is asking us to pay—and so far the lessons have all been neat and tidy, laid out like mosaic tiles in an artist's workshop. The real-life investment process, however, is far from neat and tidy. Unlike the artist, we usually don't start with a well-ordered collection of tiles. Instead, they come through the door randomly, sometimes arriving in batches and other times only in broken bits and fragments.

In this chapter, I'll explain how I put the pieces of two stocks together to arrive at buy decisions for two core holdings in my portfolio. Be advised, however: in my experience, playing with the pieces and trying to put them together results in a compelling idea only about 10% of the time. If you're doing your investment research with proper diligence and high hurdles, roughly nine out of ten companies you look at won't qualify. Something will be wrong with the business, or the management will be off, or—most likely, because you'll be looking at high-quality companies—the price will be too high. That's okay. In fact, that's desirable. If your initial research to idea hit rate is high, it likely means that you're not looking at enough companies, or that you're being too lenient on the ones you are looking at.

Given that business quality is the main driver of investment results, it's usually best to start there. Every case is different, however, and your process should be flexible rather than doctrinaire. As you'll see, I have discovered compelling investments beginning with each of the three BMP variables.

ALPHABET

The Business

When I began to look at the company as a potential investment in early 2016, like most people, I regularly used many Google applications. Reading the company's 2015 annual SEC filing, however, I learned something that I didn't know: at the time, Alphabet owned seven different platforms with more than 1 billion users. These included not only Search, maps, Chrome, YouTube, and Gmail but also Android and its Google Play app store as well. Since then, it has added four more, which like the rest are largely free to customers.

Clearly, Alphabet's engineers have a genius for building everyday products that everyday people use. Amazon has only one offering with more than 1 billion consumer users—Amazon.com—and Facebook has only three: Facebook itself, Instagram, and WhatsApp. Facebook, however, acquired the last two by the time they'd gained critical mass. Alphabet, by contrast, bought Android before it had a single user, and it bought YouTube when it had only sixty-seven employees.

After it acquired Android, Google executives made the decision to give the software to cell phone manufacturers for free. Low-margin hardware makers got their phone's operating system for nothing, while Alphabet got the opportunity to sell games and other high-margin apps in its Play Store. Today, Android has nearly 2 billion users; its software powers two-thirds of the world's cell phones; and its market share is growing. Habituated to a free operating system, most of the world's handset makers will find it hard to wean themselves off Android. Android thus has multiple moats. It's the low-cost provider of smartphone software—it's harder to get a lower cost than free—it has a trusted brand, and the switching costs for both manufacturers and consumers are high.

YouTube, if anything, is even more of a formidable business. It has more than 2 billion regular users and is the go-to platform for anything from music videos to plumbing tips. YouTube generates one-third of all daily mobile internet traffic, which is an incredible statistic—more than three times that of Facebook. Even six years ago, when I began to study it, YouTube on mobile alone reached more young American adults than any legacy television network, broadcast or cable. Most important, YouTube is a perfect example of network effects. With more viewers by far than any other online video platform, YouTube attracts the most ad dollars, which it shares with the people who produce music videos and plumbing tips. This revenue sharing incentivizes more content generation, which attracts more users, which attracts more ad dollars, and so on and so on as the flywheel keeps spinning.

When I began looking at Alphabet, however, these business segments were small in comparison to Google Search. This was less a reflection on them than it was on the gargantuan nature of Search itself. It makes all online enterprises, except for perhaps Amazon, look small.

Starting from their Stanford dorm room in the mid-1990s, founders Larry Page and Sergey Brin figured out how to make their search engine not only the world's fastest but the most relevant as well. From the beginning, Page and Brin knew that the key to developing an edge in search lay in giving users answers that most directly answered their queries. Other search engines served up results based on how frequently the keyword you searched for appeared on a web page; if you typed in "penguin," and there was a web page that repeated only that single word—"penguin penguin penguin penguin penguin penguin penguin penguin"—this web page would appear at the top of your search results. Recognizing the error in logic, Page and Brin based their algorithm not on how many times a site mentioned "penguin" but on how many other sites linked to the site. The more that other websites referenced a penguin site, they reasoned, the more that site was likely to be relevant to those interested in penguins.

By 2004, Google had a market-leading 35% share of all American search queries, but every year Page and Brin put time and money into making Google Search ever faster and more relevant. They were throwing sharks and alligators into Google's moat. In 2010, Google Search executive Amit Singhal typed in "mike siwek lawyer mi" for a visiting reporter from *Wired* magazine. The top result listed an attorney, Michael Siwek, who practiced in Grand Rapids, Michigan. Then the engineer typed the same query into Bing. Top links included ones to football safety Lawyer Milloy, but none having to do with Mike Siwek, attorney at law.

By 2011, Google's share was 65%; by 2020, its share was greater than 90%; and today, Google Search represents perhaps the most powerful example of network effects ever seen. With more people visiting Google than any other search engine, Google attracts the most ad dollars, which it uses to further improve its search engine, which attracts more users, which attracts more ad dollars, and so on and so on as the flywheel keeps spinning. These network effects give Google a huge edge; Charlie Munger says he's never seen such a wide moat as Google's, and he's ninety-eight. Over the last decade, Microsoft spent nearly $15 billion trying to build Bing into a competitive threat. Even Amazon tried but couldn't break Google's grip. Beginning in 2003, Bezos hired some of the best minds in search; according to Brad Stone's *The Everything Store*, Bezos threw an enormous tantrum when the team leader left a few years later—to join Google. "Treat Google like a mountain," he has told his staff. "You can climb the mountain, but you can't move it."

Microsoft and Amazon wanted a piece of Google's action so badly because search is likely the internet's mightiest and most profitable toll bridge. Search is, quite literally, the gateway to the information superhighway. Amazon may control e-commerce, but physical goods account for only 25% to 30% of economic output. Services accounts for the other 70% to 75%, and services is where Google excels. Anyone in the world who wants a divorce lawyer, a mortgage broker, or information on a Caribbean vacation Googles it, which means that every divorce lawyer, mortgage broker, and Caribbean-related travel business must advertise on Google. The best part is that advertisers don't mind paying Google, because advertising on its site is both cheaper and more effective than advertising on traditional media. When a travel agent or a divorce lawyer advertises on TV or in the local newspaper, they're unsure their message will reach its intended audience. On Google, advertisements are tied to keywords, so advertisers can measure whether their spending is effective or not.

As impressive as all this was, as I continued to read about Google, I was startled by how immature digital advertising was. Google was already so pervasive and so profitable in 2016 that it was natural to assume the online market was penetrated, but the facts argued otherwise. Digital spending the year before represented only 25% of the world's total ad spend. Because Google's market share of digital ad spend was roughly 60%, Google's total share of worldwide ad spend was therefore only 15%. Therefore there was little question that Google could grow to multiples of its size. If you included adjacent media like direct mail and in-store promotions, Google's share was less than 10%. At its zenith, before radio and television encroached, print advertising was 80% of total worldwide ad spend.

The same dynamics—small share, large market, competitive edge—held equally true for YouTube and Android. YouTube competed in the same online advertising market that Google did, while Android would inevitably grow as its users spent more money through their phones on games and other apps.

Given all this, you'll understand why, by the time I'd finished my initial inquiry into Alphabet's business quality, I was paying full attention. It's rare to find a single billion-user digital platform with moats around it and decades of growth ahead. Alphabet had at least three.

The Management

It was obvious from the start that Alphabet's management was a liability—or was it an opportunity? I couldn't be sure, which brings up an important point about the BMP process. As I said at the beginning of this chapter, the checklist is theoretically neat and clean, but in reality it's messy and ambiguous. Few management teams are as obviously excellent as Amazon's. Sometimes management may be owners but not act like long-term ones; they may be milking the business. Sometimes management tries to act like owners, but they don't really understand what drives value creation. Such was the case at Alphabet, and it confused me. Page and Brin were brilliant engineers, and it was clear that they genuinely cared about the long-term health of their company. But they were not financially sophisticated at all. This presented a quandary that I needed to work through.

In an industry where playful cultures are common, Page and Brin have established one of the most outrageously undisciplined. When Charlie Munger visited Google headquarters, he said at a Berkshire meeting, it looked like a kindergarten. ("A very rich kindergarten," Buffett interjected.) Page and Brin obviously assumed that if the company led with compelling products, money would naturally follow—but at times Alphabet seemed to deliberately aggravate those who cared about dollars and cents. An entire segment of Alphabet is called "other bets," which when I began to study the company included speculative ventures like Project Loon, a network of balloons launched into the stratosphere to bring the internet to remote parts of the world.

What struck me while researching Page and Brin was that they were excellent at introducing billion-user applications but, aside from Search, they were terrible at monetizing them. I could tell that from looking at Alphabet's 2015 profit margins. With the ultimate toll bridge onto the internet, the company should have been among the most profitable of all the software-based tech platforms; instead, its margins were among the lowest. Facebook, which ran a similarly capital-light toll bridge, was posting 40% operating margins. Alibaba, the Chinese internet giant, went public with nearly 50% operating margins. Alphabet's operating margins were only 25%.

This made no sense: Alphabet's revenues were five times greater than both Alibaba's and Facebook's. How could its margins be 15 to 25 percentage points lower? Once you write the software and buy or rent the servers to do the computing, every incremental sales dollar comes in at nearly a 100% margin. Software, in the jargon of tech, "scales" like no other business. Yet Alphabet's peers, with lower sales, had higher levels of profitability.

The blame for this, I came to learn, was entirely Page's and Brin's. They had always been less interested in money than in engineering challenges, and once they became multibillionaires they became even less interested in the former and more in the latter. Unlike the Mendelsons and Tom Murphy, they loved their business so much that they didn't have the objectivity required to systematically grow its value. To their credit, Page and Brin realized this about themselves early; only three years after founding Google, they named veteran tech executive Eric Schmidt as CEO. This, they said, would give the company "adult supervision." Then they retreated into their engineering laboratory to solve problems like aging.

A decade later, however, Page took back the CEO title, and while he engaged for a time with the mundane aspects of running the company, he soon lost interest again. According to later reporting by *Bloomberg Businessweek*, his eyes would glaze over when meetings involved business rather than technological issues. When a Google employee was explaining something to Page that didn't hold Page's interest, Page told the employee, "What you do is boring." The small group of executives who reported to him came to be known as "AlphaFun" and often worked on pet Page projects that had little commercial potential.

In 2013, Page stopped taking part in product launches and earnings conference calls; two years later he officially acknowledged his indifference by establishing a holding company called Alphabet.

This was potentially wonderful news! Under the new structure, Page and Brin ceded day-to-day control of the company's major platforms—Google, YouTube, Android, and its emerging cloud business—to a nonfounder. That left Page free to pursue moonshots.

Meanwhile, the person who would now be in charge of the company's truly commercial products was Sundar Pichai, a wunderkind from modest circumstances. Pichai had grown up in southern India, where he and his brother slept in the living room of their family's apartment. To get around town, he, his brother, his mother, and his father rode together on a Lambretta scooter. When Pichai was twelve, his father bought the family's first telephone, but they didn't need a phone book, because Pichai memorized every number his family ever dialed.

To my mind, Pichai's promotion materially changed the management equation. Now we had someone in charge who was not only smart, but also hungry. As I read more about him, Pichai struck me as someone intently focused on using his engineering chops to make money. One of his first coups inside the company had been to find a way to monetize Google Earth, of all things.

Of course, Pichai wasn't in charge of the entire operation—yet. Given Page and Brin's progressive pulling back from day-to-day operations, however, I felt it was only a matter of time before Pichai got the full reins.

What would happen to Alphabet's profitability with a hungry executive like him in charge? The answer to that question made my abstract idea about earnings power suddenly concrete. Given its subpar margins and its superior businesses, Alphabet could easily double its earnings more or less immediately with a management team that was more aligned with shareholders.

Several months before Pichai's appointment, Page and Brin had already taken a step toward reestablishing adult supervision by naming Ruth Porat, a former Morgan Stanley executive, as the company's chief financial officer. Within a year, the former Wall Street banker had bought back $5 billion of stock, which was a good capital allocation move, especially since that money might otherwise have gone to moonshots.

Combine Pichai's technical brilliance and immigrant drive with Porat's financial savvy, I thought, and Alphabet's financial statements could soon reflect that they owned the highest-caliber collection of businesses on earth.

The Price

While working through the "M" in the BMP analysis had proved tricky, the "P" was extremely easy. It didn't take much imagination to see how Alphabet's earnings power was much greater than its current, reported earnings. The gap between its reported 25% operating margin and its earnings potential was so big you could drive a truck through it.

In mid-2016, I counted three ways in which Alphabet's reported margins didn't accurately reflect its underlying business quality:

1. Facebook and Alibaba, both online toll bridges like Alphabet, had 40% to 50% operating margins, as previously mentioned. There was no way that Alphabet, which had five times more revenues, was inherently less profitable than they were.

2. The only other segment that Alphabet disclosed besides core Google was its other bets segment. According to the company's annual SEC filing, these other bets lost $3.5 billion in 2015. Back these losses out of Alphabet's income statement, and the margins rose from 25% to 30%.

3. Although YouTube and Android were not disclosed as separate reporting segments, it was an open secret on Wall Street that both were losing money despite their phenomenal business attributes. Under Pichai, it seemed inconceivable that both would languish as money losers for much longer. Android controlled the guts of two-thirds of the world's mobile phones. YouTube generated one-third of all mobile internet traffic. How could these businesses fail to turn a profit? Unless someone repealed the laws of business and finance, sooner or later their business quality would shine through.

Taking all these facts into account, I assigned a 40% operating margin to Alphabet, in line with Facebook's. As the following table shows, this made the price attractive even on the company's prior year revenues. If I projected the company's revenues three years out, I was pay-

Alphabet's earnings power, 2015

In billions, except per share data	Reported	Earnings power	
Revenues	$75	$75	Margins adjusted to
Operating margin	25%	40%	align with Facebook's
Operating income	$19	$30	
Tax rate	17%	17%	
Net income	$16	$25	
Shares outstanding	0.7	0.7	
EPS	$23.11	$36.97	
Stock price	$735	$735	
Cash per share	($97)	($97)	
Net price	$638	$638	
P/E multiple	28x	17x	

Source: company SEC filings

ing an even cheaper price. As you can see from the next chart, my 2018 earnings power for Alphabet was roughly $64 per share, nearly triple its actual 2015 earnings. The multiple the market was asking me to pay was therefore not twenty-eight times but one-third that, or nine times.

At the time, the average stock sold for roughly twenty times earnings. The market was thus allowing me to purchase some of the best businesses on the planet for half the price of an average business. That struck me as a good deal. I backed up the truck and made Alphabet a core position.*

---

* Purists may object to removing Alphabet's excess cash from its quoted market price in my exercise. Here again, as in all things, I followed my common sense rather than a doctrinaire formula. Unlike many businesses, Alphabet needs little cash to run its operations, so its cash is therefore extraneous. Not only that, but under new CFO Porat, the company had begun to return cash to shareholders. Note, however, the point I made in chapter 8 regarding materiality. If you don't like my adjustment, fine—don't back the cash out from Alphabet's stock price. This changes the entry multiple from nine times to twelve times, and the earnings yield from 11% to 8%. The adjustment doesn't change the conclusion that, in mid-2016, Alphabet was a compelling buy.

Alphabet's earnings power, 2018

In billions, except per share data	2015 actual	Earnings power	
Revenues	$75	$130	Sales grow 20% per year, in line with historical growth rates
Operating margin	25%	40%	
Operating income	$19	$52	Margins adjusted to align with Facebook's
Tax rate	17%	17%	
Net income	$16	$43	
Shares outstanding	0.7	0.7	
EPS	$23.11	$63.89	
Stock price	$735	$735	Cash on balance sheet grows 20% per year in line with sales
Cash per share	$97	$168	
Net price	$638	$567	
P/E multiple	28x	9x	

Source: company SEC filings

Postmortem

By 2018, Alphabet's earnings had doubled from 2015, but its reported profit margins had declined as the company continued to invest in new initiatives, including a push to catch Amazon in cloud computing. This doubling of earnings is a long way from the tripling I'd projected as earnings power—but remember, earnings power is not a profit forecast or an earnings estimate. It's an attempt to articulate a digital company's eventual moneymaking potential.

Despite this margin degradation, Alphabet's stock outperformed for the first three years after I bought it, as the market continued to give Alphabet credit for its growing revenues and its strong set of superior businesses. Then, in late 2019, Alphabet announced that Sundar Pichai would take over as CEO of the entire holding company, replacing Page. Shortly after this announcement, Pichai received the world's biggest stock and option grant since Tim Cook took over from Apple's founder, Steve Jobs. The headlines said that Pichai's grant was worth $200 million, but that estimate relied on all sorts of fuzzy assumptions. The real story was that Pichai, who had owned 18,000 Alphabet shares prior to his promotion, now owned nearly thirteen times more. He was now a real owner, and all signs were that he was prepared to act like one.

While the stock has been a consistent outperformer since I bought it, as you can see from the chart below, the share price started to really pick up after Pichai took over. He and Porat have improved profit margins, bought back big chunks of Alphabet's stock, and closed several of the company's moonshots. Project Loon is now dead, and Alphabet shares have more than doubled, easily beating the market.

Of course, it was not clear when I bought the stock that Page and Brin would hand the company over to Pichai. The truth is, however, that Alphabet's many businesses are all so clearly superior that its stock would likely have continued to outperform no matter who was in charge. Remember: business quality trumps management quality. As Buffett has famously said, "I try to invest in businesses that are so wonderful that an idiot can run them, because sooner or later, one will."

Total return since Sundar Pichai took over Alphabet

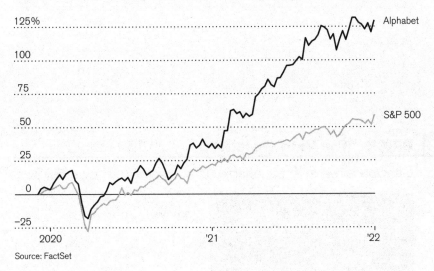

Source: FactSet

Business Management Price (BMP) Checklist

1 BUSINESS QUALITY CHAPTER 6

Does the company have a low market share...?

...In a large and growing market?

And a sustainable competitive advantage?

2 MANAGEMENT QUALITY CHAPTER 7

Does management think and act like owners?

Do the executives understand what drives business value?

3 PRICE "The Veto Question" CHAPTERS 8 AND 9

Can you arrive at a reasonable earnings yield—ie, over 5%?

| **Yes** As they say on Wall Street, back up the truck. If you're right on B, M, and P, you're in for a good long ride. | **No** Wait and watch. |

ALPHABET, 2016

	YES	NO
Yes. In 2016, digital advertising was 25-30% of total ad spend. Google had roughly 60% of this, so Google had a ~15% share of the worldwide ad market. At its peak, print advertising was 80% of total ad spend.	✓	
Yes. Global ad spend is roughly $500 billion. Factoring in other media spend like direct marketing, which Google can address, the market is closer to $1 trillion. Both businesses grow in line with worldwide GDP.	✓	
Yes. Search is a classic network effects business. Google built the fastest search engine with the most relevant results. This attracted users, which in turn attracted advertisers, which gave Google more money to reinvest in search, which made it an even better search engine. The flywheel was born.	✓	
Yes and no. Page and Brin are brilliant engineers with a knack for creating billion-user products. On the other hand, "ownership" to them does not equal wealth generation. This creates problems for their fellow owners.	✓	✓
Yes and no. Page and Brin love playing in the tech sandbox. However, in 2016 there were signs they would allow non-founders to run things, and these managers were financially savvy.	✓	✓
TOTAL	**4**	

BMP SCORECARD	
4 or 5 out of 5	**Could be a great long-term holding. Proceed to PRICE.**
3 out of 5	**Wait and watch. "Nos" could become "yesses."**
0 to 2 out of 5	**Likely not a candidate for long-term investment. Reject.**

Yes. If in 2016 you applied Facebook's margins to Alphabet and forecast revenues three years out, you arrived at an earnings power yield of 11%. This is a great yield for one of the world's best businesses.

INTUIT

I was introduced to Intuit by an excellent *Fortune* article in late 2017 by Geoff Colvin, who profiled a company that dominated two large, consumer-oriented markets: tax preparation software (TurboTax) and small-business accounting software (QuickBooks). What especially drew my attention was Colvin's depiction of Intuit's management team. Knowing how fast technology changed, they had a history of disrupting themselves, as Colvin put it, "without the motivation of a crisis." It's rare to find a forty-year-old software company whose markets aren't mature and whose management isn't set in their ways, but it was clear from reading Colvin's piece that Intuit was such a company. It constantly introduces new products, improves existing ones, and, when conditions warrant, abandons those that no longer work.

Intuit's executives measure everything, and they encourage a culture of transparency that's shockingly honest. TurboTax's business leader, Sasan Goodarzi, once tried to engage in some old-fashioned rent seeking by raising prices without offering customers anything in return. Goodarzi was forced to backtrack. "I own this decision," Goodarzi told his peers, according to *Fortune*. "I had no idea this would happen, and I'm sorry to you all." Rather than fire or demote Goodarzi, Intuit's outgoing chief executive made him Intuit's new CEO.

Any company that conducted itself like this deserved a closer look, I thought—especially one that owned two dominant software platforms.

With Alphabet, business and price were the easy variables, while the management question was tough. The research on Intuit was different. It wasn't difficult to check the boxes on business quality and management quality, but the price the market was asking me to pay befuddled me for some time. As a result, I had to watch and study the company for nearly two years before I finally got comfortable with the *P.*

The Business and the Management

The more I studied Intuit, the more obvious it became that it made no sense to study *B* and *M* separately. They were too tightly intertwined. Intuit was founded in the 1980s by Scott Cook, who learned how to give consumers what they wanted while working for Procter & Gamble. Intuit's first product was a DOS-based program called Quicken, which soon came to dominate the market for personal-finance software. In the early 1990s, when Intuit introduced a version of Quicken on Windows, Cook and his team were surprised to learn that it was being used as much in the office as at home. At first, Intuit executives thought people were balancing their personal checkbooks while at work, but it turned out that they were using Quicken to run their small businesses.

Other small-business accounting programs, it turned out, were not as user-friendly as Quicken. Thus was born QuickBooks, a specialized package that can accomplish all the back-office needs of a small business without any of the encumbrances of double-entry bookkeeping. "We built an accounting product that didn't seem to have any accounting," Cook told *Fortune,* and it became a hit.

But Intuit didn't stop there. It invented and brought to market TurboTax, which, thanks to its user-friendliness, became the leading personal-tax prep program. In the late 1990s, Intuit introduced QuickBooks Online, which didn't require a customer to buy a disk in a box, and a decade later it enabled the product to work with mobile phones. International versions followed and, in 2015, so did a version for self-employed gig workers that the company bundled with TurboTax.

Cook is long retired as CEO, but he remains Intuit's largest individual shareholder and chairman of the executive committee. He did not object when, in 2016, his successors sold Quicken, the original product that he had introduced to put Intuit into business.

Today, Intuit is composed of two distinct businesses inside a single corporate entity: TurboTax, which is largely mature, and QuickBooks, which is far from it. TurboTax already helps 30% of all Americans file their tax returns. With its brand name and marketing muscle, Turbo-

Tax is like a Value 2.0 company. It has a moat but not a small market share, and it grows slowly and steadily, grinding profits higher like a leading consumer brand should.

Unlike most consumer products, however, TurboTax is used only once a year. Small businesses, on the other hand, use QuickBooks every day to keep their beans counted. It is therefore a much stickier business, with much higher switching costs. For a customer to quit QuickBooks, he or she would have to rip the guts out of his or her back office and start over with a new one.

QuickBooks has other moats, too. It has three times more subscribers than its next-largest competitor, Xero, which gives it advantages in both brand and scale. More subscribers mean more revenue than the competition, which means more ammunition to spend on marketing and R & D. When I studied the small-business accounting space in 2018, Xero spent $235 million annually to market its product and develop improvements to it. Intuit spent $2.8 billion, or twelve times more.

Such a dramatic spending advantage guarantees that QuickBooks will not only hold its market share but also grow it. With more marketing dollars to advertise and more R & D dollars to improve the software, how can there be any other outcome?

In many ways, QuickBooks' advantages of brand plus size and scale are identical to Budweiser's fifty years ago. There's one important difference, however. In the late twentieth century, Bud was selling into largely saturated markets; in the early twenty-first century, QuickBooks is just getting started. Intuit estimates that, worldwide, 800 million small businesses and self-employed people could one day use QuickBooks. But in mid-2019, QuickBooks had 4.5 million subscribers. This meant that less than 1% of potential subscribers were subscribed to the accounting program that was so easy it didn't seem to have any accounting in it.

Many companies exaggerate their "total addressable market," or TAM, and while doing my research I found this to be true of Intuit. After poking around small-business and self-employed statistics online, I decided that QuickBooks' TAM was closer to 200 million worldwide. Though a big haircut from Intuit's 800 million estimate, 200 million potential subscribers meant that QuickBooks reached only 2% of them. That was still not a lot!

The Price

In September 2018, Intuit traded for $225 per share, or nearly fifty times its prior year's reported earnings. Unfortunately, the stock looked expensive even when I made adjustments to arrive at a reasonable earnings power. I loved the business and the management, but in Value 3.0, price has veto power. I knew that if I overpaid for Intuit, as with any business my returns would be mediocre. So I watched and I waited.

Every time Intuit reported earnings, I read its quarterly report. In the fall of 2018 and again in 2019, I tuned in to the company's highly informative analysts' day, which Intuit broadcasts live online. Nearly two years later, the stock looked attractively priced—but not because it was cheaper. It was because I realized something I hadn't earlier.

As I'd done with Alphabet, in my initial earnings power exercise I had projected Intuit's revenues several years forward. I had also adjusted Intuit's margins from 25% to 40%, which was about what Bennett Stewart's EVA analysis would suggest its margins were once you capitalized the company's marketing and R & D spend. I didn't feel comfortable assigning Intuit the 60% margins I'd derived when I made the apples-to-apples comparison with Campbell's. That felt overly aggressive; Intuit wasn't going into harvest mode anytime soon.

Sometime in late 2019, however, I realized that I had approached the initial earnings power exercise too simplistically. As I later did with Amazon, I drilled down deeper.

Like Intuit itself, QuickBooks was two distinct businesses under one umbrella. There was the desktop version of QuickBooks, which legacy businesses used and loved and wouldn't give up no matter what the enticement, and then there was QuickBooks Online, which ran on the cloud. While the former was mature, the latter was anything but. QBO, as the product is known, is the perfect product for the times, a mobile application that's as easy to use on a smartphone as it is on a PC. Because of this, and because of QuickBooks' advantages in marketing and product development spend, Intuit was doubling QBO subscribers roughly every two years. And yet, it still had only 2% of its addressable market.

When I projected Intuit's revenues the first time, I had merely carried forward Intuit's historical ten-year revenue growth rate of 9%. But QBO was becoming a bigger and bigger part of Intuit's business mix. In 2015, QBO had generated 15% of total corporate sales; in 2019, when I looked at Intuit again, QBO generated 25%; and if current growth rates continued, in a few years QBO would represent 50% of all corporate revenues.

This had two important investment implications. From a quantitative perspective, as QBO became a larger part of the company, Intuit's growth would accelerate. In terms of business quality, QBO's outsized growth meant that the best part of Intuit's business, the one with huge moats and only a single-digit share of its potential market, was becoming an increasingly important part of Intuit. QuickBooks Online was to the Digital Age what Buffett used to call Coke and Gillette at the height of Value 2.0—an "inevitable."

This was the key insight I'd missed before: QuickBooks Online was going to become a juggernaut, and when it did, it would move Intuit's sales and earnings growth trajectory materially upward. This didn't occur to me initially because I was still making the transition from financial analyst to business analyst. I was looking at the numbers first, with the business in the background, so to speak. When I correctly put QBO in the foreground, it became apparent that I needed to make the following adjustments to Intuit's income statement:

- I grew QBO subs 30%/year, slower than its 35% to 40% historical rate.

- I grew the average revenue per QBO subscriber 9%/year. This is consistent with historical averages and consistent with Intuit's push to turn QBO into a platform—one that sells customers ancillary services like payroll, invoicing capability, and the like.

Intuit's earnings power

In millions, except revenue per customer and per share data	Actual 2019	Estimated 2022	Projected growth rate	
QuickBooks Online				
Market potential (number of businesses)	200	212	2%	
Penetration rate	2%	5%		
Online subscribers	4.5	10	30%	
Average revenue per subscriber	$370	$481	9%	Adjusted operating margin between its existing 25% and its optimal 60% to a directionally accurate 40%.
Online revenue	$1,663	$4,791	42%	
Other revenue (TurboTax etc.)	$5,121	$6,142	6%	
Total revenue	$6,784	$10,933	17%	
Operating margin	25%	40%		Reduced share count by 3% per year based on management's history of share buybacks.
Operating income	$1,854	$4,373		
Tax rate	16%	16%		
Net income	**$1,554**	**$3,665**		
Shares outstanding	264	237	–3%	
EPS	**$5.89**	**$15.44**		Because Intuit's earnings power is 2.5–3x its reported earnings, the stock is trading for 19x, not 51x.
Share price	**$300**	**$300**		
P/E multiple	51x	19x		
Memo: QuickBooks Online revenue as a percentage of total	**25%**	**44%**		

Sources: company SEC filings

- I grew Intuit's other, more mature businesses, like TurboTax and QuickBooks Desktop, at 6%/year, consistent with historical averages.

- I moved Intuit's operating margins from 25% to 40% as discussed above.

- I reduced the share count by 3%/year. This assumption was derived from my observations of management. Financially savvy, Intuit's executive team had a history of reducing the

Business Management Price (BMP) Checklist

1 BUSINESS QUALITY   CHAPTER 6

Does the company have a low market share...?

...In a large and growing market?

And a sustainable competitive advantage?

2 MANAGEMENT QUALITY   CHAPTER 7

Does management think and act like owners?

Do the executives understand what drives business value?

3 PRICE "The Veto Question"   CHAPTERS 8 AND 9

Can you arrive at a reasonable earnings yield—ie, over 5%?

Yes As they say on Wall Street, back up the truck. If you're right on B, M, and P, you're in for a good long ride.	**No** Wait and watch.

INTUIT, EARLY 2020

	YES	NO
Yes. Its core product, Quickbooks Online, which helps small businesses balance their books, has 5 million subscribers. The marketplace is ill-defined, but is anywhere from 200 million to 800 million potential users.	✓	
Yes. In addition to the stats above, Intuit's mobile, cloud-based solution competes mainly against legacy ways small businesses manage their receipts and collections. Major competitors are Excel and the shoebox.	✓	
QuickBooks is embedded into a small business' daily workflow, making it hard for a business to switch to a competitor. Moreover, with more cashflow than any rival, Intuit can plow back more money than others into both sales and research and development.	✓	
Yes. Founder Scott Cook and current executives own stock worth more than $4 billion—they have a lot riding on Intuit's future. More than just ownership, Intuit executives have shown the ability to evolve from "software in a box" to slick mobile solutions that make customers' lives easier.	✓	
Yes. Management has shown several clear markers of financial sophistication. Intuit executives measure everything, including customer acquistion cost in relation to ultimate revenue generation.	✓	
TOTAL	**5**	

BMP SCORECARD	
4 or 5 out of 5	**Could be a great long-term holding. Proceed to PRICE.**
3 out of 5	**Wait and watch. "Nos" could become "yesses."**
0 to 2 out of 5	**Likely not a candidate for long-term investment. Reject.**

When I understood that QuickBooks Online was soon going to become the company's main product, I could see that I was paying less than 20x Intuit's near-term earnings power.

share count over time. Like Tom Murphy at Cap Cities, they knew that every dollar of cash not needed to grow the business should be returned to shareholders. This improves return on capital while simultaneously increasing every shareholder's pro rata ownership of the company.

With the earnings power multiple now under twenty times, I felt comfortable buying shares at $300. As you can see from the BMP checklist, business quality, management quality, and the price the market was asking me to pay were all excellent.

Postmortem

The pandemic arrived after I bought Intuit, and the stock briefly dropped into the low $200s. While I'd like to report that I backed up the truck and bought more, I didn't. I was too busy buying Amazon's stock, foraging for masks and toilet paper, and trying to remain rational while Mr. Market was going nuts.

It's worked out fine, however. As I write today, Intuit's business continues to thrive post-pandemic. QuickBooks Online now represents 30% of total corporate sales, and Intuit's stock price has nearly doubled from where I bought it two years ago.

CHAPTER 10

Investing in Non-Tech Companies

I've spent the bulk of this book arguing that technology stocks are where the money is, but the irony is not lost on me that the first bread crumb on the trail to this discovery was HEICO, a decidedly non-digital company. HEICO's low-cost advantage, coupled with its small share of a huge market, crystallized for me the wisdom of targeting only companies that had both moats and exponential growth potential. It just so happened that when I overlaid this template on companies I was studying in the early twenty-first century, 90% that fit the framework turned out to be tech.

Ten percent, however, were not tech. I own businesses that help people fly, paint their houses, and gain access to credit, and this chapter will introduce you to a few of them. More importantly, it will help you identify promising non-tech companies on your own.

When looking at old-economy companies, your template should be the same as when you're looking at new-economy companies. As a reminder, it's:

> A small share of a large market, coupled
> with a sustainable competitive edge
>
> +
>
> A management team that thinks like owners
> and knows how to drive business value
>
> +
>
> A price that gets you under twenty times
> earnings power, for a 5%+ earnings yield

When considering non-tech, however, we must ask several additional questions. Digital companies often deliver some combination of faster, better, and cheaper, so it's best to assume that tech is gunning for whatever non-tech business you're studying. "Guilty until proven innocent" may not be a sound judicial principle, but it's a prudent one when it comes to investing in legacy industries.

Here are three questions that I use to help me separate vulnerable non-tech companies from ones that should prosper in the Digital Age. In conjunction with these three questions, I introduce three companies that answer the questions in the affirmative.

1. IS THE PRODUCT THE COMPANY MAKES TECH-PROOF?

In my experience, this is the most fruitful place to start in non-tech—with a business model that naturally resists the trends associated with the Digital Age.

All my non-tech companies are largely tech-proof, but none is more so than Sherwin-Williams. You just can't render paint digitally, at least not yet. Meanwhile, there's something deep within human beings that drives them to coat their walls, either for decoration or to for protection against the weather. Early paints were made with oil and water but also included seashells for texture and berries for pigmentation. As time went on, techniques for making attractive and durable coatings became closely guarded; in 1502, English craftsmen formed a guild called the Worshipful Company of Painter-Stainers.

Painting got off to a slow start in the United States thanks to the Puritans, who in 1632 charged a Massachusetts man for building a house containing "excessive wainscoting and other adornments." American practicality eventually prevailed, however, and in 1866 Henry Sherwin and Edward Williams founded the company that would introduce the world's first guaranteed ready-to-use paint.

As the Industrial Age progressed, "paint" became "coatings" and was used to finish anything that needed protection from the elements—automobiles, ships, and airplanes. Sherwin-Williams developed many of these modern finishes and patented them, then kept investing money into research and development to deepen its product moat. To make the Sherwin-Williams brand instantly recognizable, it also kept spending on marketing.

Today, Sherwin-Williams has competitive advantages that stem from 150 years of innovation and brand loyalty, but what really distinguishes the company is its incredible retail presence. Sherwin-Williams operates a network of nearly 5,000 company-owned stores. Its nearest competitor, PPG, operates roughly 1,000.

Why does this network of owned stores give Sherwin such an edge? Because only Sherwin-Williams has a store base extensive enough to touch American painters every day. Like many great businesses, Sherwin-Williams created its moat by asking, "What does my customer care about?" and then working backwards. Until computers learn how to coat buildings, the economics of house painting will remain simple: 80% of a painter's expenses are labor, and 20% is paint. Time is therefore money to a painter, and Sherwin-Williams focused on that fact like a laser beam. Given these unit economics, wouldn't painters reward the company that saved them time? If so, why not roll out so many stores that most would drive by them every day on their way to the job?

That's what Sherwin-Williams has done. They even offer free curbside pickup, so the painters don't have to get out of their trucks, and free donuts as well. The company supplements this network with a fleet of 3,000 trucks whose drivers make constant runs to jobsites to replenish low supplies. PPG owns their stores, but with roughly one-fifth the number of Sherwin-Williams's, PPG doesn't have the density required to make the network ubiquitous. Benjamin Moore has more contact points, but because these outlets are independently owned rather than under Benjamin Moore's corporate umbrella, they don't operate as a unit. Only Sherwin-Williams can handle national accounts, and only Sherwin-Williams can roll out a new and improved finish in a consistent, nationwide brand campaign. Only Sherwin-Williams has a mobile app that allows a painter to order ten gallons of eggshell white in the evening, then show up at his local store the next morning and find it ready for him.

Sherwin's store network gives it an edge, and this edge is growing. Every year, Sherwin adds nearly one hundred new company-owned stores; PPG's annual new store count barely reaches double digits. Little wonder that Sherwin-Williams is growing its North American paint sales at 6% to 7% per year, twice the rate of the competition.

Meanwhile, Sherwin-Williams has a low share of a large and growing market. The worldwide painting and coatings sector remains fragmented, and Sherwin has only about a 10% share of it. At nearly $150 billion in annual sales, the market is huge and growing slightly more than the worldwide economy.

Management is also excellent. Unlike Bezos at Amazon or Murphy at Cap Cities, there is no single star executive; there is, however, a culture at Sherwin-Williams that inculcates in every employee, from the lowest store trainee to the CEO, the discipline of thinking like an owner. Unlike many companies, Sherwin doesn't just leave it to the CFO to understand principles like return on capital and capital allocation.

You can tell this not only from how executives talk but how they act. Sherwin-Williams rarely buys companies, but when they do, they do it brilliantly. In 2017 it bought Valspar, a leading industrial coatings company, using 100% debt financing. Like Tom Murphy at Cap Cities, they reasoned that they didn't need to use stock; instead, they could use Sherwin-Williams's ample cash flow to pay down the debt over several years, then enjoy the acquisition forever, without any dilution to shareholders. Unlike other, less disciplined businesses, Sherwin-Williams articulates clear priorities for its cash flow and then sticks to them. It reinvests money in its store network, in product development, and in the Sherwin brand; anything left over goes back to the shareholders, either as dividends or as share buybacks.

2. IS TECH MAKING A SUPERIOR BUSINESS EVEN BETTER?

If it hadn't been founded in 1899, Equifax could rightly be categorized as a tech company. The product it sells, consumer credit information, is nothing but numbers.

Most people know their FICO score; fewer know that Equifax is one of only three companies that produces the raw data used to determine that score. The company was founded by two brothers, Guy and Cator Woolford, who went door-to-door in Atlanta at the turn of the century asking businesses about their customers' propensity to pay their bills on time. The Woolfords would note the responses in a ledger, lumping them into general categories like "Prompt," "Slow," or "Requires Cash." Then the brothers would go back to the office, compile these figures in a book, and publish them in something they called *The Merchant's Guide*. Although copies cost $25—a lot of money back then—many Atlanta businesses felt it was worth it: knowing a customer's credit history before extending credit to him or her was valuable indeed.

Thus was born the modern American credit bureau, an enterprise that's evolved from the analog *Merchant's Guide* to one now existing in the digisphere. The business model, however, has remained the same. Potential creditors, mainly banks and other financial institutions, give Equifax and its two major competitors, TransUnion and Experian, data on their consumers. The credit bureaus slice and dice the data in ways much more sophisticated than "Prompt," "Slow," or "Requires Cash," then turn it around and sell it, often to these same financial institutions.

Anytime your major customers give you critical raw materials for free and then buy it back from you once you've improved them, you've got a good business. Moreover, this business is protected by sizable barriers to entry. Equifax and its two major competitors have each been in business for generations; banks are habituated to doing business with them; and because banks gain valuable insights thanks to the bureaus' analytics, they aren't interested in providing the same raw credit data to a new entrant for free. Meanwhile, the credit bureaus enjoy the same kind of digital economics as Google, Facebook, and the rest. Their product is nonphysical—it's just zeros and ones—and every time a financial institution pays to access that data, the incremental profit margin to Equifax approaches 100%.

Credit bureaus have also proved surprisingly tech-proof. Numerous fintech start-ups have tried to estimate a customer's propensity to service their debts by examining their social media accounts, but it just doesn't work as well as looking at a customer's actual credit history. While consumers may be sensitive about who sees their data, nearly all Americans want creditors to view it—otherwise, they couldn't get a loan. One financial services start-up catering to younger investors thought it could attract customers by promising not to share their credit data with the bureaus, but their customers rebelled. Without this data, they couldn't get a car loan or a mortgage.

In 2017, however, Equifax allowed something to happen that justifiably outraged consumers. Hackers breached the company's IT system and stole the credit data of nearly 150 million people, or almost half the American population. Worse, many of these records involved the "big four" security identifiers—name, address, birth date, and Social Security number. The CEO "resigned," and in the end, the company agreed to pay almost $1 billion in fines and class action settlements.

The stock tanked after the breach, and I bought it, thinking that Mr. Market was giving me an opportunity to buy a superior business at a reasonable price. Although the breach was bad, it was likely not going to cripple the company. One of corporate America's dirty little secrets is that fines and class action suits are just a cost of doing business. Nobody wants to pay out hundreds of millions of dollars, but these settlements usually amount to only a year or so of annual earnings. Once paid, they disappear. Meanwhile, the great business carries on.*

As usual, a few years later, Equifax had sorted through its breach issues. It had hired new IT administrators; it had paid its fines; and it had hired a new CEO, one who used the crisis as an opportunity to double down on tech.

It's rare to find a superior business such as Equifax, and it's even more rare to find a superior business that's getting better—but Equifax is one of them. Already protected by high barriers to entry, Equifax is using tech to accelerate its revenue growth, its profit growth, and, most important of all, its competitive edge.

To do this, however, Equifax must invest—a lot. The company is spending roughly $1.5 billion over the next several years to move its data from in-house servers, essentially giant computers, to Google's cloud platform. While this has depressed its short-term earnings, Equifax's long-term earnings power will be materially higher once the migration is finished. Costs will be lower, while the data offerings to Equifax's customers will be more robust and therefore more valuable.

Like many tech companies today, Equifax is tanking short-term earnings to grow long-term ones. This scares off short-term investors who look at current price/earnings multiples, but to longer-term shareholders, it's a thing of beauty. Conceptually, it's like the fines Equifax had to pay. Once the spending is done, it's behind Equifax, but the improvement to the company's earnings power will remain.

---

* Interestingly, of the nearly 150 million identities stolen, not one was used to buy anything. As is so often the case with such hacks, the invaders were spies, not thieves. In early 2020, the U.S. Department of Justice indicted four Chinese military officers for the crime. Apparently, China believes that somewhere in Equifax's data it can find a four-star general who has both sensitive intelligence and an embarrassing credit history.

3. IS THE BUSINESS SERVING THOSE THE DIGITAL REVOLUTION HAS LEFT BEHIND?

The name Dollar General is misleading: it's a general store, but it doesn't sell everything for a dollar. Instead, it sells staples like bread and eggs in small stores conveniently located for lower-income people in both urban and, especially, rural areas. Dollar General is an amazing company and a misunderstood one. It does well by doing good—although, unfortunately for the United States, the need that the company fulfills continues to grow.

Dollar General embodies all the qualities I've written about regarding Equifax and Sherwin-Williams. Like paint, the corner store is tech-proof. No online retailer, not even Instacart, can match the convenience of popping in after work when you need a few things for the evening meal. Like Equifax, Dollar General is one of the rare enterprises today whose business is getting better, although, as I say, for all the wrong reasons.

Dollar General is tech-proof largely because of its convenience aspect, but it's also tech-proof because its customers can't afford Amazon Prime's $139-a-year subscription. The annual income of a Dollar General customer is roughly half that of the average American's, and it's common to see posters in Dollar General stores that say, WE ACCEPT THE SUPPLEMENTAL NUTRITION ASSISTANCE PROGRAM, a reference to the federal program formerly known as food stamps. To understand Dollar General's unit economics is to enter into the world of the nation's have nots. I once went on a Dollar General store tour with a company executive who explained why the company sold Welch's juice for kids' lunchboxes in plastic bottles with resealable caps rather than the standard juice boxes. The resealable caps, he explained, allowed the child to bring the bottle back home so that his or her mother could reuse it, diluting new juice with water for the following day's lunch.

Some progressives criticize Dollar General for adding to the nation's nutrition crisis by stocking lots of Little Debbie snack cakes and relatively few fresh fruits and vegetables. But such critiques miss the root cause of the problem. Dollar General didn't create food deserts; they're responding to them. Often, the company opens a store after a Target or a Kroger has shut down. In such communities, the alternative to a Dollar General is nothing, and nutritionists now credit its stores for marginally improving poor people's diets by offering brown rice, beans, and whole-wheat bread. "I've come around," public health professor Elizabeth Racine told *Bloomberg Businessweek*. "I appreciate that they are willing to operate in low-income places because so many other stores aren't willing to go there."

As the de facto monopoly store for many small communities, Dollar General could easily follow the example of earlier general stores and gouge their customers. Dollar General, however, does not. Instead, it tries to stay within 3% to 5% of Walmart's prices, an amazing feat when you consider that Dollar General has less than one-tenth of Walmart's buying power and that it must maintain a network of tiny stores, often in the middle of nowhere. The company's return on capital runs around 20%, which indicates a superior business but not a predatory one. Indeed, Dollar General sets its prices at a 40% discount to two of its major competitors, the CVS and Walgreens drugstore chains. The last time I checked, a gallon of Silk almond milk costs $4 at a CVS but $2.50 at Dollar General.

Walgreens and CVS count on convenience to draw customers, but Dollar General counts on both convenience and price, and by putting itself on its customers' side, Dollar General is prospering. While the drugstores have been struggling to maintain sales momentum, Dollar General has grown same-store sales, those from its existing store base, for thirty-one consecutive years. Sooner or later, as my old newspaper mentor Pat Stith used to say, you get to be known for who you are.

With only 6% of Walmart's sales, Dollar General has a low market share of the huge U.S. retail market. It has multiple competitive advantages: low cost, convenience, and the trust of its customers. Sadly, demand for its stores also continues to rise as the nation continues to bifurcate between well-educated, digitally literate urbanites who have crossed the industrial divide and those who have not. American cities are filled with postindustrial knowledge workers in fields like marketing, media, finance, and, of course, technology. Parts of these cities, however, remain poor and disenfranchised, and vast stretches of rural America have been decimated by the offshoring of American factories.

Dollar General is placing its stores in these empty spaces, and every year the white space grows. Five years ago, Dollar General estimated that the entire dollar store industry could support 10,000 additional locations. Even though the industry has added thousands of stores since then, Dollar General now thinks the nation could support 12,000 more. As the digital divide accelerates, so does the demand for Dollar Generals.

PART III

Putting It All Together

CHAPTER 11

Buy What You Know— With a Twist

Many people ask me where I get my ideas, and the implication seems to be that it's hard to find them, but the opposite is true. Because I've been hunting for good investments every day for more than twenty-five years, the challenge is not to source ideas but to triage them. Still, when I began my stock-picking career, I remember asking myself the same question you may be asking yourself: Where do I begin? There must be a river of ideas out there somewhere, I remember thinking, a river I could jump into and let the current take me away. I was right— but because I was new, I didn't know where it was.

To help you find it, I'll start by giving you the same advice that Peter Lynch gave me through his books a generation ago: Start with what's right under your nose. Don't take your experience for granted; tap into it. Tapping into your own experience will lead you to at least one idea worth researching. While that one might not work out, it will lead you to two others, which will lead you to a human source who tells you about several more, and so on. If you proceed like this, one day you'll find yourself in the flow, happily fighting to keep your head above water.

As you begin your search for compelling investments, you should use both your personal and your professional experience. Both are valuable, though for different reasons, and both have specific strengths and weaknesses that we'll explore now.

USING YOUR OWN EXPERIENCE
IN THE WORKPLACE

Familiarity breeds contempt, so you're probably unaware just how much of an edge you have in your everyday work life. You understand better than 99% of other investors which companies are thriving and which aren't in your own little corner of the economy. Buffett calls such industry expertise a "circle of competence," and using this circle to source investment ideas can be very rewarding.

Not many of us like to admit it, but professional investors envy those who are embedded in a particular economic sector. While in time we may develop a circle of competence in a few different industries, the pros understand economic sectors the way an outsider understands a town that he visits but does not live in. As an inhabitant, you know the good neighborhoods and the dangerous ones. You know the shady characters and the solid citizens, and this knowledge gives you an edge.

Peter Lynch lamented that instead of applying this edge, most amateur investors take it for granted. "In general, if you polled all the doctors," he wrote in *One Up on Wall Street*, "I'd bet only a small percentage would turn out to be invested in medical stocks, and more would be invested in oil; and if you polled the shoe-store owners, more would be invested in aerospace than in shoes, while the aerospace engineers are more likely to dabble in shoe stocks." This was wrongheaded then and it is even more wrongheaded today. The rapid pace of technological change right now makes your knowledge more valuable than it would be during periods of economic stability. When the pace of change is fast, the gap between industry experts and the rest of us widens.

So embrace your circle and mine it for ideas. If you work in sales and marketing, you understand Salesforce better than nearly every investment professional. Is Salesforce widening its moat, or is someone tunneling under it? Is there room for nimbler, niche entrants in the large and lucrative market of customer relationship management software? I don't know—but you probably do.

The same is true for other business-to-business companies such as Autodesk, Splunk, and Ansys. If you work in industrial design and use computer simulation software to test prototypes of your new products, you'll know better than almost anybody whether Ansys has a moat or not.

When it comes to companies like Salesforce and Ansys, which sell only to other enterprises, there's one important caveat: in general, customers of these so-called business-to-business, or "B-to-B" companies, feel much less loyalty compared to customers who are individual consumers. Unlike companies that sell to individuals, B-to-B companies often cannot rely on consumer preference, customer habituation, or the power of their brand. The business-to-business market is driven by price and performance, which makes a B-to-B company's edge much more difficult to maintain.

Faster, cheaper, better—this is all companies in the B-to-B space care about. Branded moats do not exist in the B-to-B ecosystem; most often, a company's edge is like HEICO's: it is the low-cost producer of an essential product. Even then, you should be wary of a low-cost moat, because rivals are almost always busy trying to breach it.

Because of this, your insights in the B-to-B realm will be actionable only if you can assure yourself that the moat of the company in question is deep and durable indeed. My friend Henryk, an auditor who I regularly play poker with, recently asked me if I knew about a company called Alteryx. Alteryx makes tools for accounting firms and other companies that need to organize and analyze large numerical datasets. I didn't know Alteryx, but I asked Henryk a few questions about it. Is it the market leader? Yes, he answered. Can you imagine doing your job without it? Absolutely not, he said. While Alteryx isn't the low-cost producer, he explained, the cheaper products on the market are materially inferior. Most importantly, the productivity payback to his company when using Alteryx is enormous, and Henryk couldn't see any competitor improving on it. Only when I heard those answers did I encourage him to pursue the idea further.

USING YOUR OWN EXPERIENCE AS A CONSUMER

Researching consumer-facing tech companies is the opposite of burrowing into your workplace niche. Billions of people use Apple's and Alphabet's products every day, so most people on Earth understand how they work and how important they are. This common knowledge makes it harder for us to gain a value-added insight into them.

Gaining an edge here, however, is not impossible. When it comes to consumer tech companies, we must often look a level or two deeper.

Everyone knows that Amazon is the leader in e-commerce, and most understand that smaller, independent merchants use Amazon's platform to sell goods. But fewer people realize that many such merchants resent paying the steep fees Amazon charges them, so they turn to Shopify. Shopify makes software that allows small businesses to create their own virtual storefront. On Shopify, merchants can do most everything they can on Amazon, but for a lower fee. Some call Shopify "the anti-Amazon," and its plug-and-play alternative has done very well indeed for both customers and shareholders. Shopify shares have appreciated fortyfold since its IPO nearly seven years ago.

Similarly, most people know that Netflix dominates video streaming, but fewer have focused on the fact that Roku dominates the market for the devices that connect Netflix to our TVs. Roku began as an undifferentiated piece of hardware, but it's turned its market-leading middleman position into an early twenty-first-century toll bridge. Roku now has so many devices installed in homes that it's forcing streaming channels to share a cut of their subscription fees or risk losing their place on Roku. The stock market has taken notice: Roku's stock has dramatically outperformed the larger market since its IPO four years ago.

Even the best-known tech companies can occasionally be hiding in plain sight. Often it takes a market meltdown to give you such opportunities. In the dot-com bust, I was able to buy Apple, Ben Graham–style, for the liquidation value of its assets. In normal markets, earnings power can be an important tool to help you uncover such value. Everyone knows Amazon is a dominant business, but fewer understand that it's attractively priced, too.

The term "digital divide" is used to describe how technology has benefited wealthier, more educated people and left poorer, less educated people behind, but a digital divide exists between the generations as well. Older investors have been trained by people like Peter Lynch to invest in the stock market, and they have been well rewarded for it. But when it comes to the new digital economy, they have received no such training. Younger investors couldn't be more different. They understand technology because they've been born into the Digital Age; they don't need any training here. Scarred by three different market crashes, however, younger investors distrust the stock market in a way not seen since perhaps the Depression.

As a result, older and younger investors each have gaps in their knowledge that impair their ability to see the full investment picture. "Buy what you know" therefore comes with a twist. As I said in the introduction, older investors understand markets but not technology, while younger investors understand technology but not markets. Until both groups mend these gaps, neither will be equipped to profit from today's economic dynamism.

COMMONSENSE ADVICE FOR YOUNGER INVESTORS

Look at the data and be rational.

Given the market meltdowns you've lived through and the state of your financial health, you have cause to be mistrustful of "the system." For those who are deep in college debt and often with little to show for it, there are legitimate reasons to believe that the United States is not a meritocracy and that the game is, generally speaking, rigged.

It would be foolish, however, to let such experiences carry you away into the irrational land of meme stocks and Dogecoin. There may be money to be made in cryptocurrency (more on this in chapter 12), but before you head to that exotic frontier, I encourage you to familiarize yourself with the data from the U.S. stock market, which over the last one hundred years has generated more wealth than any other single place in history. I know it doesn't feel like it, but the data show that the market has been an excellent place to invest even over the last turbulent generation. Since 1988, the midpoint of the Millennial birth years, the stock market has appreciated roughly 11% a year despite its many ups and downs, materially better than the S&P's hundred-year average of 9%. The value of American real estate, your other major legacy investment choice, has appreciated only 4% annually since then. If you'd put $10,000 into real estate in 1988 without using any debt, it would be worth around $35,000 today—but if you'd put that money into a stock market index fund, it would be worth nearly ten times more. If you'd identified superior businesses that beat the market, you'd have done even better.

I admit that investing in the stock market can occasionally be jarring. At the onset of the coronavirus pandemic, the stock market declined 30% in less than a month, the quickest such downturn in history. During such times, it's natural to be frightened. But these are precisely the times you need to stay rational and remember Ben Graham's friend Mr. Market. During such times, ask yourself: What is the stock market? Then answer: it's a place where over time, value gets found out. If you internalize this mantra, market pullbacks are simply times when you can buy great businesses on sale.

You know tech; now master technique.

Your intimacy with tech gives you an edge, but this edge is actionable only if you know how to exploit it. It's not enough to be generally familiar with tech; you must understand what moats to look for and the traits that characterize a good management team. You also need to be familiar with basic valuation tools so that you can identify not only great businesses but attractively priced ones, too. This is what Part II is all about. It's the guts of the Value 3.0 stock-picking process, and if you've skipped ahead in the book, I encourage you to go back and read it.

It's also important for you to tune out the static of modern, digital life. One of the undesirable things about being born into the Digital Age is the stimuli you're bombarded with. My generation was taught to read the morning paper and watch the evening news; today, information comes from your phone like water from a firehose, and it won't stop unless you stop it. So turn it off, or at least filter the information so that only the intelligent bits reach you. Otherwise, you'll end up with a head full of data that, to use an engineering expression, is 100% noise and 0% signal.

One of your main distractions is the "gamification" of investing, led by youth-focused stock-trading platforms like Robinhood. Robinhood has grown fast by marketing a slick app using advertising campaigns featuring young people saying things like "I'm a broke college student and investments might help my future tremendously." Wait, as the Millennials like to say, what? I have no problem stipulating that investing is a game; that's part of what makes it fun and challenging. But it's a particular type of game, and to misunderstand its nature will lead you to misplay it. Investing is not a game in the same way that roulette is a game; it's not a game of chance, and winners and losers are determined not in a matter of minutes, days, or even months. Investing is a long-term game, one that rewards skill, strategy, and, above all, persistent effort over many years.

Of course, it's a free country and a free market, and you can play the investing game any way you want. But more fortunes have been built trying to get rich slowly than trying to get rich quick. The bulk of the latter attempts end in disillusionment and disaster. Another former board boy, Jesse Livermore, was what we today would call a day trader. Livermore was such a talented speculator that, before he was twenty, he was banned from all the stock brokerages in Boston. Livermore made fortunes during the panic of 1907 and the crash of 1929 by shorting stocks, or betting against them, but he also went bankrupt more than once when his speculations failed. In 1940, rather than face another personal financial crisis, Livermore took a Colt pistol and shot himself in the head in the cloakroom of the Sherry-Netherland hotel.

Don't be this guy. No matter what you invest in, adopt the same patient, disciplined mindset that all value investors have adopted since Ben Graham invented value investing more than a century ago.

COMMONSENSE ADVICE FOR OLDER INVESTORS

Get to know tech.

If you're old enough to have read Peter Lynch's investment books when they came out, I don't need to convince you to put your money in the stock market. Lynch taught us that the market is the best place to grow our wealth over time, especially if we can identify superior businesses. Since his books were published, however, the internet, social media, and the cell phone have all been born. The Shiva-like nature of digital enterprise, creating new industries while destroying old ones, has rendered many of his best examples of winners obsolete.

If we are to prosper over the next generation, we must acknowledge this fact—but if you're like me and of a certain age, you resist doing so. Some of this stubbornness is understandable and even rational—investing in great Value 2.0 businesses like Coca-Cola and Pfizer has worked. It's hard to change, especially when changing means learning a new industry, a new vocabulary, and an alien business culture. Older generations are accustomed to doing business in suits and ties and corner offices. These kids wear hoodies and bring their dogs to work. Square's CEO wears a nose ring. How can we take such people seriously?

While this thinking is natural, it's also wrong. The companies run by such "children" make money—lots of it—and these hoodied software engineers preside over the most powerful economic engines ever created. Coca-Cola has been around for 135 years and has never earned more than $10 billion in a year. Alphabet, a company so altruistic that it began life as a public company in 2004 with the motto "Don't be evil," earns more than four times what Coke makes.

These are the sorts of statistics that make Buffett and Munger marvel at the new economy. Although they own only one major tech company, Apple, it's clear they've studied the digital ecosystem. Buffett is more than ninety years old, and Munger is nearing one hundred. If they can learn about it, so can we.

Suffer the little children.

To familiarize ourselves with tech, we're going to need some help from the younger generation. We must overcome our natural resistance here as well. We don't understand technology in the native way that our children do, and this makes us feel inferior. Worse, it makes us feel old. These feelings compound until many of us dismiss technology as an asset class that we can invest in.

To avoid such a trap, we must open ourselves to lessons from the younger generation. Often these lessons will come randomly and indirectly, and you should be on the lookout for them. Buffett said he understood Apple's power as a consumer brand only when he took his great-grandchildren and their friends to Dairy Queen. The kids were all so absorbed by their iPhones that Buffett couldn't get them to focus on what kind of ice cream they wanted. Buffett did a lot more research on Apple after that, of course, but from this initial insight came an investment that's made Berkshire Hathaway more than $100 billion in unrealized gains so far.

I understood Chegg, the nation's leading online textbook provider, only when my son's friend Meraz explained it to me. When I was in college, we bought our textbooks at the university bookstore. If we were enterprising, we got them from someone who'd taped a flyer to a lamppost advertising used textbooks. Today, Chegg uses the internet to rent or sell books, both new and used, and in either physical or digital form. With a leading share of the online market, Chegg has parlayed its brand name recognition into a platform for other school-related products and services. You can hire a tutor and you can join a calculus or biology forum to get answers to your homework questions. You can even find a summer internship—for a fee, of course.

Chegg might have a nonsensical name, but when it comes to serving students, Chegg is all business. Today, Chegg's revenues are roughly equal to legacy textbook provider Houghton Mifflin Harcourt, but this is a static and therefore misleading statistic. The larger truth is that over the last five years Chegg's revenues have tripled, while Houghton Mifflin Harcourt's have declined nearly 30%. Because the market recognizes that Chegg's future is bright while Houghton Mifflin Harcourt's is bleak, Chegg's market value is nearly twice that of its legacy competitor's.

The digital world is a different world, but it's an intelligible world, and one that our children and our nieces and nephews and their friends can explain to us. For this to happen, you need to allow those you've taught to become your teachers. Making that adjustment can be difficult, but once you overcome your initial sheepishness, you may find it enjoyable. I went through this process myself with my own son, a twenty-six-year-old software engineer. He used to mock my half grasp of tech, needling me for fumbling to understand what came naturally to him. Intergenerational tension ensued—but at some point I decided to drop my defensiveness and learn from him. Once I did, my understanding of tech materially advanced.

CHAPTER 12

Thoughts on Process and Priorities

In your hunt for superior investment ideas, you know where to begin: use your own experience. You also know how to finish: run those ideas through the BMP checklist. But what do you do during the time between the start and the finish? What of the long, indeterminate middle? And after you make your investment decision, what then? Putting the question another way, what should the process of a successful investor look like in the early twenty-first century?

Like gardening, meditation, and raising children, investment research works best when you approach it in a constant and methodical way. Investing does not reward sporadic, stop-and-start activity, so it's best to get yourself into a rhythm. As any gardener, meditator, or parent will tell you, everyday discipline is the key.

In that spirit, here are some practical suggestions to help you establish solid habits that I have found buttress my investment practice. Later, in the second part of the chapter, I will give you some thoughts on a few of the more popular—and dangerous—"trends" that threaten to distract you from your goal of being a disciplined wealth-builder in the early twenty-first century.

1. *"Be quick—but don't hurry."* This is a great quote from John Wooden, the legendary college basketball coach. It's pertinent to life in general and investing in particular, especially if this book has generated some enthusiasm in you. When you get that first bright idea, don't be in a hurry to invest all your money in it. Instead, apply the same rigorous, patient process that value investors have used since Ben Graham. Put the idea through the various filters of the BMP checklist, then take care not to let your exuberance influence your judgment.

As an investment analyst, you should be like a scientist: cool and analytical. When Darwin was formulating his theory of evolution, he paid more attention to the data points that contradicted his thesis rather than the ones that affirmed it. He knew that only by being tough on himself could he build the strongest possible case.

2. *Extend your circle of competence—and don't be shy about it.* Profiting from the digital economy begins by tapping into your own experience, but it shouldn't end there. You should tap into others' experience as well. Test out your insights with others. Friends, relatives, coworkers—all of them can help you with both idea generation and investment conclusions. If you're in sales, ask your colleagues whether they see the same moats in Salesforce that you do. If you're in accounting and you like Intuit's products, ask your colleagues if they agree.

It's also important that you not limit your inquiries only to the people you know. Do a little investment research when you go to trade shows or industry conferences. Ask people there what trends they're seeing; pick brains and compare notes. These investigations will help you gain conviction, either positive or negative, about your idea.

If you approach the research process in this way, over time the power of compounding will kick in, but instead of money that compounds, it will be both your knowledge and your circle of contacts.

3. *Read—a lot.* There's a reason Buffett guards his calendar so jealously: he blocks out hours in his day to read, and you should follow his example. A deep knowledge of the investment landscape depends upon regular engagement with newspapers, periodicals, online blogs, company reports, trade magazines, and books about business and investing. Reading helps you enter and then remain in the river of ideas, which is important both for idea generation and for staying informed about the stocks you already own.

4. *Use Mr. Market to your advantage.* I wouldn't advise waiting for a crisis to invest in a good idea. If the business is right, the management is right, and the price is right, then the time is right as well. Buffett nearly lost See's Candies by haggling over a few million dollars, and he lost Walmart in its early days because he waited for the stock to tick a fraction lower.

When Mr. Market offers you a wonderful business for a bargain price, however, it's time to pay attention and likely also time to invest aggressively. This is easier said than done. I've lived through numerous mini-crashes and three major market crashes in my career, and I can tell you that it's never easy putting money to work when the news is uniformly bad. "Reinvesting when terrified" is how Jeremy Grantham accurately describes the process, and over time you should train yourself to learn how to do it.

It will help tremendously if you internalize the fact that while every market crisis is different in its details, the narrative is essentially the same: the world is coming to an end. The financial system is going to collapse, or the coronavirus is going to halt all human activity forever. Nonsensical in hindsight, these story lines feel very real at the time. Such narratives present intelligent investors with a dramatically easy decision tree: either the world is in fact coming to an end, or we're going to muddle through. So far, it's always been the latter, which means that, so far, investing while terrified has been the right approach.

5. *Regarding constructing a portfolio, my best advice is: Don't.* Buffett has pooh-poohed modern portfolio theory and its tenet of diversification. So has Peter Lynch: "diworsification," Lynch called it, and he's right. A diversified portfolio of one hundred mediocre stocks will produce nothing more than a diversified, mediocre result.

Rather than diversify, I recommend that you use your edge to find businesses with edges. Identify a few companies that pass the BMP test; buy them; and then stick with them like my friend Alex stuck with Apple. Conviction trumps fear, and with conviction you won't need to be worried about being overly concentrated. The world has changed a lot since Andrew Carnegie built his steel empire, but one of Carnegie's cardinal principles has not. " 'Don't put all your eggs in one basket' is all wrong," he told the graduating class of Curry Commercial College in Pittsburgh in 1885. "I tell you, 'Put all your eggs in one basket, and then watch that basket.' "

6. *Find your tolerance for concentration and calibrate accordingly.* Some people just can't abide the stress that comes with putting all their eggs in one basket and then watching that basket. Many people aren't like Alex. They don't have the confidence to put their entire life savings into a few high-conviction stocks, and that's fine. Knowing where on the "eggs in the basket" spectrum you fall is part of understanding your temperament as an investor, and that's very important information to have.

So figure out your tolerance and invest accordingly. Often this comes only through real-world experience; only when you own something will you know how terrified you feel when it drops 30%.

To jump-start the process, however, you might take a sheet of paper and write down how much you have in retirement savings and how much extra money you have to invest after normal living expenses. Ask yourself: What percentage of each do I feel comfortable putting into a few high-conviction stocks? Play with the numbers. Perhaps it's 70% of your retirement money but only 25% of your discretionary brokerage money, or perhaps the numbers are reversed. Whatever the numbers, settle on a figure and then see how it feels as time goes on. You'll find the right balance over the years.

Whatever amount that doesn't go into individual companies should go into either an S&P index fund or (my preference) a tech-focused exchanged-traded fund (ETF) or a tech-focused mutual fund with a superior long-term track record. The latter approach will increase your chances that the returns on your non-concentrated pool will still be above average.

7. *Either way, do as Peter Lynch said and did: Invest for the long run and invest incremental dollars regularly over time.* One of the principal reasons Lynch had such faith in amateur investors is that, unlike professionals, they don't have to report short-term performance to anybody. This exemption allows everyday investors to keep their eye on the horizon and focus on great businesses that can grow and compound for years. As a professional, I can tell you that what Lynch said is absolutely true. It's very hard to balance the prospect of an idea that might work in three years' time against the prospect of it harming performance over the next three months. Amateurs face no such quandaries, and you should take advantage of this fact. If you stay on top of your high-conviction investments and remain convinced they are sound, then you can ride the market's inevitable ups and downs. Even better, underspend your income and put money to work in the stock market every pay period. Such regular additions are like snow added to a snowball rolling downhill. The snowball is already naturally growing and compounding as it goes, but the added snow makes it grow and compound even faster.

PRIORITIES

As long-term investors, our priorities should be clear: we need to make steady, disciplined endeavors to identify, buy, and hold superior businesses. Such businesses will not be lottery tickets of speculations; if we want to buy a lottery ticket, we should go to our local 7-Eleven. To risk a material part of our wealth on a game of chance when we understand how to invest intelligently is like having an affair when we're in a happy marriage. Just as we can never take back our infidelity, we can never make back the money we have lost while speculating.

Unfortunately, there are lots of such extramarital possibilities to distract us in the early twenty-first century. These temptations will lead us away from our real purpose, which is to build long-term wealth in a reliable way.

Of course, we shouldn't reject all new opportunities out of hand. The world is changing, and we should be open to developments beyond just those in publicly traded tech companies. Whether it's cryptocurrency, meme stocks, or socially responsible investing, I try to evaluate such trends just as I would any other opportunity: rationally. What follows are some initial conclusions I've drawn regarding them and some advice about how, as a disciplined investor, you might want to approach them yourself.

Cryptocurrency

In the early spring of 2020, on the day that turned out to be the absolute bottom of the pandemic crash, I bought an inconsequential amount of Bitcoin. I was curious about how cryptocurrency worked and whether the experiment was likely to end in tears. By buying some Bitcoin, I was implementing a saying an old boss of mine used to toss around: "Buy a little," he'd say, "and see how it feels." It's good advice. Buying something makes an abstract investment idea very concrete—because now you own it.

Eighteen months later, my Bitcoin investment had sextupled. Am I proud of my Bitcoin buy? No! While it certainly falls into the general Value 3.0 framework (the world has changed), my purchase strayed completely from the BMP template. I'm happy to have made money, and my Bitcoin has done better on an annualized basis than Intuit, Amazon, Alphabet, and all my other Value 3.0 investments. But that's noise, not signal. Buying Bitcoin was like buying a lottery ticket, whereas the BMP template is deliberately constructed to keep you and me focused on finding ways to *systematically beat the market*. The quality of the business, the quality of the management team, and the price the market is asking you to pay—that's all that matters, and all that has ever mattered.

That said, I am not one of those old-school value investors who reject cryptocurrencies out of hand because they're new. The biggest, including Bitcoin itself, have already passed the first hurdle that any new currency needs to clear: it's been accepted by the public. However, while there's likely lots of money to be made in crypto, I don't think the enduring wealth will come from any of the currencies themselves. It's going to come instead from those companies that facilitate the cryptocurrency ecosystem—that make crypto faster, cheaper, and easier to use, just as Alphabet, Amazon, and the rest make the internet faster, cheaper, and easier to use.

While it's still early days between me and crypto, here's a summary of what I've learned so far, along with what I believe the implications should be for your investment priorities going forward.

What are cryptocurrencies? The first ones were designed as a new method of payment, one that's anonymous and encrypted and builds on itself in a database called a blockchain. This blockchain improves on the legacy system of financial transactions in many ways. There are no costs, no middlemen, and therefore no prying eyes to see how you and your counterparty are transacting business. All of these are powerful arguments for using alternative currencies like Bitcoin.

On the other hand, the whole idea behind cryptocurrency as a medium of exchange is entirely circular. When someone executes a blockchain transaction in a particular cryptocurrency, he or she gets a "coin" that has no inherent value. But the coins must have value, or there will be no incentive to execute and verify transactions on the blockchain. Thus, to begin the virtuous circle for a particular cryptocurrency, enough people must agree that the coin is worth something. If they do, more and more people will do the work required to make the blockchain function.

A cryptocurrency is the ultimate flywheel, in other words, and it's entirely dependent on an intellectual imputation of worth. If not enough people believe that a cryptocurrency's tokens have value, then there's no inducement to go looking for them. And if nobody goes looking for them, the blockchain won't function.

Many find it absurd to impute value onto something that was created a little more than a decade ago. This newness doesn't bother me, however; the truth is that the value of all currencies, new or old, is imputed. Why has gold been hoarded, plundered, dreamt of, and used as a medium of exchange for centuries? Because in the distant past, our ancestors discovered a deposit of shiny yellow metal and said, "Wow, that's beautiful!" Different peoples in different parts of the world found different objects that, like gold, were both beautiful and rare. Cocoa beans and cowrie shells were two early popular currencies.

At some point, however, civilizations around the world standardized on gold as a measure and storehouse of value. The same metamorphosis has occurred with cryptocurrency, with one startling difference. It took our ancestors millennia to agree upon gold, but it's taken modern civilization less than a decade to agree upon Bitcoin and Ethereum.

People believe in Bitcoin and Ethereum because it enables us to conduct business with more privacy and less cost. That's a good thing—but is it an investable thing? When we boil cryptocurrency down to its essence, even if we believe in it as a medium of exchange, it's nothing more than a currency, like gold or the dollar. And all currencies, new or old, are inherently inferior investments because, unlike a business, currencies are not dynamic. Currencies are inert; they store and represent value. They don't create new products and enter new markets and thereby produce more wealth for their owners. With currencies, as Buffett says about gold, once you own one, all it does is sit in a room and stare back at you.

Early crypto adopters have made the same kind of big money that the first prospectors made during the 1849 California gold rush, but we should be happy to miss out on scores like this. Like my six-times Bitcoin return last year, they're random.

In fact, if you believe cryptocurrency will continue to thrive, you should study what happened during that gold rush. Although a few lucky miners struck it rich, most ended up penniless and heartbroken. Meanwhile, smart businesspeople built fortunes around the mania by enabling it to flourish. Levi Strauss ran a modestly successful dry-goods store in San Francisco until he bankrolled a man who'd designed a set of riveted denim pants that miners could use. John Studebaker came West as a gold miner but quickly realized he could make more money manufacturing wheelbarrows. Studebaker invested his wheelbarrow profits into a company that built Conestoga wagons and then iconic American automobiles. Henry Wells and William Fargo started a transportation company to move gold via steamship from California to New York; in 1852 they opened a branch bank in San Francisco to buy gold dust and make loans to miners. This branch became the foundation for the modern Wells Fargo banking giant.

The parallels with today's cryptocurrency movement should be clear: if you want to invest in this generation's gold rush, then you should do it by investing in this generation's versions of Levi Strauss, Studebaker, and Wells Fargo. I have no specific ideas yet, but publicly traded investment candidates already exist. Coinbase, the world's largest digital currency exchange, is one, and exchanges are inherently good businesses. If enough people use them, network effects kick in. Many other ecosystem enablers such as Coinbase are likely to follow, and these are the ones we should be paying attention to as potential investments.

Reddit and Meme Stocks

The current "meme stock" craze makes the cryptocurrency markets seem orderly and rational. What's happening on the Reddit messaging site and playing out subsequently in the stock market is much crazier than buying a single lottery ticket or having an isolated extramarital affair. It's an orgy of irrationality, a specualtive spasm that takes us back to Ben Graham's day, when men in many-colored hats gathered at the curb to trade securities. Because technology is so much more powerful today, however, the mania has been amplified and weaponized, and it will almost certainly end in tears.

The meme stock phenomenon began shortly after a mob of President Trump's supporters stormed the Capitol in early 2021, and I don't think the timing is coincidental. Both movements are characterized by a frenzied, wild-eyed worldview that has more in common with a *Planet of the Apes* movie than reality. On a Reddit subchannel called WallStreetBets, millions of amateurs with limited investment experience banded together to take on and punish professional short sellers. These hedge funds had bet against GameStop, AMC Entertainment, and others by borrowing their shares and then "selling them short." In doing so, the fund managers had no other motive except the usual one on Wall Street: to make money. They believed these businesses had a bleak future, so they sold the shares in the expectation that at some point their price would decline and they could buy them back at a lower price.

Many in the Reddit mob, however, were younger investors who'd been traumatized by the financial crisis, and they took this short selling personally. They began to funnel all their anger and frustration about "the rigged system" into destroying the shorts. Forget that hedge funds had little to do with causing the financial crisis; that was the fault of the banks and the government regulators who failed to oversee them. These people were determined to exact revenge.

While individually the members of the Reddit mob were small and weak, together they were, as they liked to say of themselves, ape strong. One claimed that there were nearly 3 million retail investors on WallStreetBets, each with an average balance of more than $6,000 "and not one boring research report in sight." Three million accounts X $6,000 average balance = $18 billion worth of ammunition, and the ape-strong mob deployed it devastatingly well. By buying en masse, in less than five months the mob drove shares of GameStop up fifteenfold and AMC Entertainment thirtyfold. This squeezed the shorts, who were betting that the shares would fall; one hedge fund that was short such stocks required a $3 billion capital injection to stay afloat.

What the Reddit mob pulled off may or may not have constituted market manipulation, but one thing is certain: as I write today, the stock prices of the companies they're backing have become completely unhinged from reality. Running one of them, AMC Entertainment, through the BMP checklist makes that plain.

In terms of the "B," the business, it's true that AMC is the market leader in the movie theater industry. But American theater attendance peaked in 2002, and the pandemic has accelerated the trend of people staying home and streaming. Meanwhile, the company owes more than $10 billion in debt and long-term lease obligations. Struggling with declining visitors and a heavy mortgage load, AMC has nearly declared bankruptcy several times in the last few years.

In terms of the "M," the management team is led by Adam Aron, an executive who's the textbook definition of a hired gun. He's been the chief executive of four public companies over the last thirty years and has never owned a material amount of stock in any of them. Aron's longest tenure was at Vail Resorts, an above-average business that owns franchise ski destinations, but during Aron's decade there, Vail's stock performed only in line with the market average. After Vail and before AMC, Aron was a senior partner at Apollo, one of the quintessential Wall Street insider firms that the Reddit mob hates so much. In late 2020, in fact, Apollo was encouraging AMC to file for bankruptcy so that as a debtholder, Apollo could gain control of the company.

In terms of P, the price the market is asking us to pay, AMC fails that test most decisively of all. The company lost money in 2020 because of the pandemic, of course, so it's impossible to value the company on current earnings. Thanks largely to its large debt load, AMC also lost money in 2019. In 2018, AMC made slightly more than $100 million, so we can use that figure, but when we juxtapose this with its market value of $15 billion, we see that AMC is trading for 150 times its 2018 earnings. That's a 0.66% earnings yield, about a third of what you can get in ultrasafe ten-year United States government bonds.

I'm happy to adjust AMC's reported earnings to get a sense of its earnings power, but what adjustments can we reasonably make to the income statement of a slowly dying movie theater chain? What trends can we count on to put fannies in all those empty seats? At the height of the AMC frenzy, *Barron's* tried to make a bull case for the stock, but even using the rosiest assumptions it couldn't get there. If revenues doubled from their peak and profits tripled, the magazine estimated, AMC would still be valued at fifty times earnings.

Fifty times is a long way from my twenty times earnings-power hurdle, and even then, getting there relies on projections that no sensible person could make. Certainly, Aron and AMC's other executives aren't making them. When AMC sold new shares to the public in May of 2021 to shore up its financial position, management included this language in its securities filing: "We believe that . . . our current market prices reflect market and trading dynamics unrelated to our underlying business. . . . [W]e caution you against investing in our Class A common stock, unless you are prepared to incur the risk of losing all or a substantial portion of your investment."

Management is giving us its own BMP analysis right there. They're telling us that the price of AMC's stock bears no relation to underlying business fundamentals. They're further telling us that AMC is the subject of so much speculation that if we invested, we could lose all our money. Worst of all, it seems that this wasn't just boilerplate language put in to appease the SEC. Around the same time management wrote these words, many executives were selling their AMC holdings.

What's so pathetic about all this, in the original sense of the word, is that many in the Reddit mob have legitimate grievances, but they are channeling their anger in the wrong direction. "I vividly remember the enormous repercussions that the reckless actions by those on Wall Street had in my personal life, and the lives of those close to me," one person wrote on WallStreetBets to explain why he invested his entire savings into GameStop. "Do you know what tomato soup made out of school cafeteria ketchup packets tastes like? My friends got to find out." To "the boomers, and/or people close to that age . . ." he continued, "Stop listening to the media that's making us out to be market destroyers, and start rooting for us, because we have a once in a lifetime opportunity to punish the sort of people who caused so much pain and stress a decade ago, and we're taking that opportunity."

As heartfelt as this plea is, there's one big problem with it: trying to use the stock market to punish people is like sending a dog to hunt for an octopus. It won't work. The market is not a public square where we can put evildoers in chains and give them a good flogging. The market is just that—a market. It's a place where the true value of businesses gets found out over time. And when AMC, GameStop, and the rest get to be known for what they are, the ape-strong warriors that own these stocks will be completely wiped out.

Socially Responsible Investing

Just as it's a bad idea to try to punish wrongdoers in the marketplace, it's also a bad idea to try to make the marketplace a forum to do good. The market is neither a moral nor an immoral place; it's an *amoral* place. Unless it's for an exceedingly discrete purpose, like selling shares in companies that did business with South Africa under apartheid, trying to do good in the stock market represents another dog-hunts-octopus kind of endeavor.

Recently, however, the Wall Street selling machine has tuned in to the fact that many people in the United States and Europe feel guilty about their prosperity and want to use their resources for another purpose besides simply building more wealth. Over the last decade, Wall Street has begun to pump out products that go by various names— socially responsible investing, ESG (environmental, social, and governance) investing, impact investing—that purport to grow your money while making the world a better place. They all have different spins, but they all share two characteristics: they manipulate your guilt, and they make above-average profits for their peddlers while delivering investors subpar returns to you.

A recent article in the *Wall Street Journal* reported that even though they cost no more than a normal ETF to run, socially responsible ETFs funds charge nearly 50% more than standard ones. At the same time, according to the paper, an analysis from the Pacific Research Institute found that putting your money into an ESG fund over the last decade would have led to performance nearly 50% lower than an S&P 500 index fund.

I'm all for making the world a better place, but these vehicles are not the way to do it. Socially responsible investing is a flimsy intellectual construct that won't achieve what you hope to accomplish. Which businesses are "socially responsible" and "environmentally friendly" and which aren't? Aside from a few obvious ones—coal companies, for example—the answer is surprisingly slippery and gray. Vanguard's socially responsible European stock fund currently holds large positions in TotalEnergies, one of the world's largest oil exploration companies, and Rio Tinto, a major copper and uranium miner. Even systematic attempts to identify companies that do well by doing good unearths bizarre candidates for investment. *Barron's* set out in 2018 to rank major American businesses by sustainability. It analyzed the 1,000 largest publicly traded companies using six outside consultancies, which ran three hundred performance indicators that were distilled into five key stakeholder categories. The winner? Clorox, whose primary product is bleach.

In this muddy world we live in, determining which companies are "good" and which are "bad" is a difficult proposition indeed. What about Bitcoin and other cryptocurrencies: Are they socially responsible? Bitcoin eliminates government and financial middlemen and it offers relief from predatory banking fees. Enthused, Elon Musk bought $1.5 billion of the currency in late 2020 for Tesla and changed his chief financial officer's title to Master of Coin. Less than a year later, however, Musk reconsidered. He decided not to accept Bitcoin for Tesla purchases until the cryptocurrency became more environmentally friendly. By mining for Bitcoin, it turns out, human beings consume as much electricity in a year as the Netherlands, the world's seventeenth largest economy. If Bitcoin continues to gain acceptance, mining for it will soon consume as much electricity as one of the world's top ten economies.

Amidst such confusion, Wall Street steps in, slaps a label on a product calling it socially responsible, and sells it as a cure-all. Caveat emptor, however: like the snake oil salesmen of the nineteenth century, those selling ESG products are lightly regulated and often don't track the efficacy of what they're selling. Nearly 70% of all private equity funds making so-called impact investments, according to the *Wall Street Journal*, aren't asking for specific metrics or reporting of any kind from their ESG managers.

Given all this, you're better off trying to identify superior businesses yourself. Not only will you likely generate better returns, but you will also naturally turn up companies that are above-average corporate citizens. Because the Value 3.0 worldview and the BMP template look to the future, they naturally filter out all sorts of companies on the wrong side of the digital divide. Fossil fuel companies, chemical companies, paper companies, defense contractors—none of these make the BMP cut, because none of them have a bright future. The *M* analysis of the executive team also uncovers potential problems. Any executive with half an ear tuned to the current zeitgeist understands that issues like climate change, child labor, and gender and racial equity are important to the customers they serve. That's why Jeff Bezos pledged in 2019 that Amazon would be carbon neutral by 2040, a decade earlier than what governments agreed to in the Paris climate accord. Dozens of other companies, including Microsoft and Uber, have joined the pledge.

This brings me back to a leitmotif of *Where the Money Is*: you don't have to rely on experts—many of whom charge a lot of money for their "advice"—to tell you what to do. Your own good judgment is enough.

Your own common sense, coupled with some diligence, will lead you to companies that are going to perform well while not adding overmuch to the world's many problems. If you feel very strongly about the issue, modify the BMP framework so that the question of good corporate citizenship has veto power. If a company that passes your BMP analysis does not clear your own socially responsible hurdle, simply reject it.

Who knows? Maybe you can perfect the process and start an ESG fund that actually delivers on what it promises. Maybe I will, too. The Value 3.0 worldview naturally lends itself to investing in responsible businesses—and today ESG is definitely where the money is.

CHAPTER 13

Regulation, Innovation, and the Second Half of the Chessboard

In roughly a generation, tech has come to dominate our economy, our daily lives—and our political discourse. Indeed, tech has gotten so big so fast that the only thing American politicians can agree on is that big tech is bad. Senator Josh Hawley, a Republican from Missouri who supported Donald Trump's efforts to overturn Joe Biden's election, recently introduced trust-busting legislation to "ban major companies in the business of offering search engines, marketplaces, and exchanges from expanding their power and creating anticompetitive conflicts of interest . . ." Elizabeth Warren, a Democrat from Massachusetts who once called Trump "corruption in the flesh," has put out press releases using nearly identical language. "It's time to break up Amazon, Google, and Facebook," one is headlined.

As an investor, such threats don't frighten me at all. Americans love a good David-and-Goliath story, which makes the narrative that big tech is bad irresistible to politicians on both the left and the right. The current chest-beating in Washington, however, is likely 90% noise and 10% signal. Headlines about regulation and breakups have so far created, and likely will continue to create, excellent buying opportunities. Mr. Market gets anxious whenever an industry faces this kind of pressure, and this anxiety induces him to unload shares at bargain prices.

There are three specific reasons why big tech has little to fear from government regulation:

- When you get past the rhetoric, the antitrust and other breakup arguments are shoddy at best and simply wrong at worst.

- To alter big tech's business model in any material way, government must break the daily habit-forming bond that exists between consumers and the world's most popular tech applications. Forged for nearly a generation now, this bond is nearly impossible for any political body to undo.

- Even if the government succeeds in breaking some of these giants up, the component parts will likely thrive and prosper. The parts may in fact be greater than the whole.

Before I get into the specifics of these red herrings, let me stipulate that I am neither an apologist nor a cheerleader for digital businesses. Instead, I try to be a dispassionate and fish-eyed analyst, and I clearly see tech's warts and flaws. I remember when Google promised that no ads would ever be sold around search results, and I've watched as that promise has been broken, first gradually and now completely. A broken promise, however, is not a broken law, and as a shareholder I applaud Google's strategy.

Likewise, I watch closely for signs that the tech companies I own are developing rent-seeking tendencies. I'm vigilant not because I'm a moralist but because rent seeking is a form of laziness. Instead of innovating on behalf of its customers, a company tries to get away with charging something for nothing—and that's bad for business. In a free-market system, this kind of behavior eventually gets found out. Intuit's QuickBooks Online is a fantastic, fast-growing product that helps small businesses keep their books in order, but Intuit executives have already confessed to engaging in rent-seeking behavior with TurboTax, the company's more mature division. I will reconsider my investment if this happens again.

Our society has laws against anticompetitive and predatory behavior, and I'm glad that they exist. Government should monitor companies and penalize abuses. It should be a tough, strong referee that ensures a fair contest and takes care that the playing field is not destroyed. Beyond that, however, government should let the players play. As a journalist, I've seen the public sector used as a tool for good, but as an investor I've seen how unskillful government can be when trying to solve marketplace problems. Capitalism is simply too open and too brutal an arena for companies to get away with abusing their customers, because the customers rebel. Often, rent seekers are punished not by the authorities but by the mass defection of consumers themselves, who abandon companies that fail to provide them with lower prices, better products, or some combination thereof.

Such dynamics are especially true today, when the pace of economic and technological change is so fast. It's popular now to pile on Google and Apple and the rest, but if they truly abused their customers, their customers would just leave.

––––––––

As to tech regulation specifically, current U.S. antitrust doctrine requires plaintiffs to prove that something called "consumer welfare" has been harmed. Usually this proof comes in two forms: higher prices or a lack of goods to choose from. Is this the world we live in today?

Google, Facebook, and WhatsApp are free, and it's hard to get cheaper than that; meanwhile, Erik Brynjolfsson's MIT study found that consumers value Facebook at $550/year, WhatsApp at $7,000/year, and Google at $17,500/year. Likewise, we are far from a world in which big tech's dominance has caused a scarcity of goods. It could in fact be argued that Amazon's "everything store" gives us so many choices that it exacerbates consumerism and environmental destruction. This is unfortunate, but it does not violate the law, antitrust law in particular.

Given such facts, a new generation of trustbusters maintains that consumer welfare is no longer the correct antitrust standard. They argue that while we can't yet see overt consumer welfare problems from Facebook dominating social media and Amazon dominating e-commerce, the government should act to prevent any possible future damage. "We cannot cognize the potential harms to competition posed by Amazon's dominance if we measure competition primarily through price and output," a twenty-eight-year-old law student named Lina M. Khan wrote in a popular 2017 antitrust article published in the *Yale Law Journal.* "[C]urrent doctrine underappreciates the risk of predatory pricing . . . [T]he economics of platform markets create incentives for a company to pursue growth over profits, a strategy that investors have rewarded."

Khan was writing about Amazon, and she is correct that Amazon has prioritized growth over profits and that investors have rewarded the strategy. That's the whole point of earnings power: to tease out the value obscured by a digital company's aggressive spending. On the other hand, Khan is breathtakingly wrong in her conclusion. To suggest that Amazon's end game is predatory pricing betrays an ignorance of how Amazon in particular, and tech in general, intends to remain successful.

Amazon is a long way from cornering the e-commerce market, but even if it were to, it would never jack up prices. Today, Amazon is one of the world's most trusted brands. To abuse this trust by starting to gouge customers would immediately and likely irreversibly impair Amazon's chances for a long and prosperous future. Amazon's value proposition is some combination of faster, cheaper, and better. It's built one of the world's most valuable companies around such tenets. Why would it ever alter them?

The general argument that big tech is no longer innovating is similarly absurd on its face. The facts make it clear that, unlike mature companies such as Wells Fargo and Coke, big tech is not sitting behind its moat and harvesting the fruits of its competitive advantage. On the contrary, big tech is spending billions every year on projects from augmented reality to the fight against aging. It's not only big tech that's innovating: the rung below is competing fiercely as well. If big tech were really quashing competition, then these lesser-known companies would not be flourishing—but they are. Shopify, the anti-Amazon that gives small merchants an alternative online presence, has a market value of $85 billion, which makes it twice as valuable as large legacy retailers like Kroger, Autozone, and Dollar General, more valuable than TJ Maxx, and nearly as valuable as Target. The number of unicorns, start-up tech companies with a day-one valuation of greater than $1 billion, has grown from only a dozen eight years ago to more than 750 today, the *Economist* recently reported.

The Democrats are now in power, however, so some form of regulation may be on the table. Lina Khan, the twenty-eight-year-old law student and Amazon critic, is now the thirty-two-year-old head of the Federal Trade Commission. Tim Wu, another academic who wrote a book called *The Curse of Bigness: Antitrust in the New Gilded Age*, is a special assistant to the president for technology and competition policy.

These officials will no doubt work to prove that big tech is indeed a menace. Meanwhile, life goes on, and billions of people continue to use big tech's products every day. It's hard to imagine how regulators can interfere with this intimate, daily relationship. Because of this, it's also hard to imagine regulators interfering with the competitive advantages—network effects, switching costs, and so on—that spring from it.

I would be more wary of regulation if the transactions that occur between tech platforms and those who use them weren't so benign. Tech companies offer services that consumers want and use; in return, consumers consent either to either pay them (Intuit, Spotify) or to monetize their eyeballs through advertisements (Facebook, Google). Critics use provocative sound bites to make us feel as if we're somehow being used and manipulated. "When you use Google to search, you're not the customer—you're the product," Dave Yost, the attorney general of

Ohio, recently wrote. That's a clever line, but in the end, my deal with Google comes down to this: after I've looked for shoes online, Google will serve me shoe ads. In return for free search, I'll make that trade all day long.

Don't get me wrong: we should continue to address issues such as privacy so that neither big tech nor big government becomes Big Brother. But as a Google consumer, I don't feel any more violated when I'm served a shoe ad than when a TV network bombards me with ads for soda and beer. I like Google's ads better, in fact, because they're served to me knowing that I'm interested in shoes.

Until it's proven that our exchanges with tech platforms are indeed sinister and harmful, our usage of such products won't change. Politicians hate to leave a fight empty-handed, however, and at the margin they may therefore win some victories, which will allow them to quit the field claiming that David has indeed defeated Goliath. But some of their proposals, and the logic underlying them, are downright nutty. Senator Hawley wants to separate Amazon's e-commerce division from its cloud-computing unit because, he claims, Amazon owns much of the technology "upon which the Internet itself is built." This assertion will come as a surprise to Sir Tim Berners-Lee, who was knighted for inventing the World Wide Web in the late 1980s, some six years before Amazon was founded and roughly twenty years before Amazon launched its cloud-computing unit.

Other regulatory thrusts seem more reasonable, and they might therefore succeed. Alphabet probably shouldn't control both online search and the world's largest brokerage for web-based ad sales. Acquiring a company to eliminate it as a rival violates antitrust law, and it appears Facebook did just that when it bought WhatsApp and Instagram. Mark Zuckerberg's 2008 email on the subject—"It is better to buy than compete"—is about as smoking a smoking gun as a regulator could hope to find.

In its core businesses, however, big tech's value proposition is so strong that there's little regulators can do. If Facebook's three apps were divested into three separate companies, as a Facebook owner you'd own three strong apps beloved by consumers. If Amazon were split into an e-commerce business and a cloud-computing division, as an Amazon shareholder you'd own market leaders in both segments. In many cases, in fact, big tech's component parts are worth more than the whole, because if a tech conglomerate were forced to separate into individual pieces, the pressure for each segment to show more than just the potential for profit would likely increase.

This logic holds for Amazon, whose cloud unit generates 10% of corporate revenues but 60% of its operating profit, and it holds especially for Alphabet. While Alphabet owns applications like YouTube and Android that have the potential to earn billions, they currently break even at best. They have been subsidized by Google Search, one of the most profitable businesses ever invented. Search is like the prize cow that gives so much milk, the farmer doesn't need to bother milking the others; if Alphabet were broken up, this would likely change. Under its new CEO, Alphabet has begun to nudge its nascent segments to higher levels of profitability, but a breakup would accelerate the process. As stand-alone entities, YouTube and Android would have to make their latent earnings power manifest.

A breakup of Alphabet, I believe, would be remarkably like Standard Oil's breakup into thirty-four separate entities more than a century ago. In 1910, the U.S. Supreme Court upheld the federal government's directive to John D. Rockefeller to dismantle the company he had built. When he heard the news, Rockefeller was playing golf with a priest.

"Father Lennon, have you some money?" Rockefeller asked the man. "Buy Standard Oil."

Rockefeller's instincts were, as usual, correct. In the decade after Standard Oil's dissolution, its component parts quintupled in value.

––––––––

Breakup risk, regulatory action of varying kinds from the new trust busters—at this point, it's all conjecture. As analysts, we should not ignore these risks entirely, but we should discount them. Until Washington produces something substantive, we should see the headlines for what they are: noise rather than signal.

What is certain, and therefore actionable, are trends right under our noses. It's 100% certain that computing power will continue to increase, and it's 100% certain that this increase will lead to more innovation and disruption. Moore's law gave us supercomputers in the 1950s, landed humans on the moon in the 1960s, put personal computers on our desks and in our laps in the 1980s and 1990s, and in the 2000s it gave us cell phones more powerful than any supercomputer. Over the last twenty years, however, it seems that tech's ambition has diminished. Its aperture has narrowed to solving problems that could be called small, and even trivial. Tech has enabled us to chat with friends, to search online for shoes, and to look for a mate without setting foot in a bar. In so doing, it has produced trillions of dollars of wealth for shareholders, but it's not produced anything you could call a major contribution to civilization. "What has the Internet done for us, really?" as Glenn Fogel, CEO of Booking Holdings, the world's leading travel website, asked recently, "except make it easier to reserve a hotel room and buy plane tickets and groceries online?"

Fogel's comment is flippant, but it's also profound, because it points to the vast possibilities inherent in the growth of computing power. Breakthrough innovations that currently lie beyond our investment horizon are fast approaching. Driverless cars, quantum computing, space colonization, practical applications of artificial intelligence, and augmented reality are only some of the developments that surely lie ahead. The compounding power of computing power guarantees it.

Futurists talk a lot about the second half of the chessboard, a reference to a likely apocryphal story first told by Islamic scholar Ibn Khallikan in 1256. The parable concerns a king who employed a court mathematician who was as intelligent as he was mischievous. One day, the mathematician proposed a game to the king.

"Let me start with one grain of wheat placed on the first square of a chessboard," the mathematician said, "and when I move to the next square, I will double the number of grains. I will continue doubling in this way until I have reached the sixty-fourth and final square. When I finish, will you grant me all the wheat on the board?"

The king, who was not good at math, agreed—only to discover that when the geometric progression was finished, he owed the mathematician 9,223,372,036,854,780,000 grains of wheat. That's 9 quintillion, 223 quadrillion, 372 trillion, 36 billion, 854 million, 780,000 grains of wheat, or nearly 1,000 times the amount of wheat grown annually on earth today.

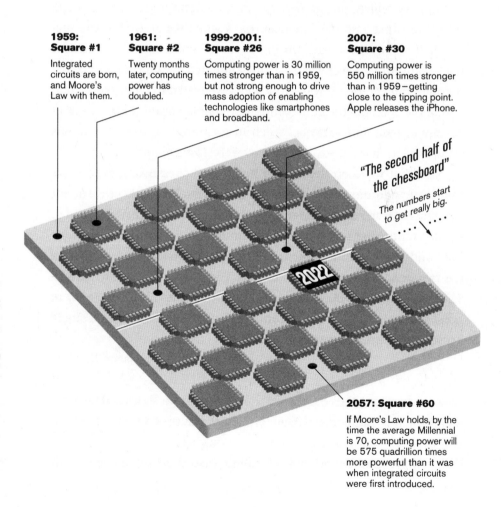

1959: Square #1

Integrated circuits are born, and Moore's Law with them.

1961: Square #2

Twenty months later, computing power has doubled.

1999-2001: Square #26

Computing power is 30 million times stronger than in 1959, but not strong enough to drive mass adoption of enabling technologies like smartphones and broadband.

2007: Square #30

Computing power is 550 million times stronger than in 1959—getting close to the tipping point. Apple releases the iPhone.

"The second half of the chessboard"

The numbers start to get really big.

2057: Square #60

If Moore's Law holds, by the time the average Millennial is 70, computing power will be 575 quadrillion times more powerful than it was when integrated circuits were first introduced.

The story illustrates why Einstein called compounding the eighth wonder of the world. Whether it concerns money or technological progress, compounding is especially wondrous when we reach the second half of the chessboard, because that's when the numbers start to get really big. Buffett had to wait until he was nearly sixty to become a billionaire, but a decade later he was worth seventeen times as much. In the sixty-three years since the transistor was first introduced, computing power has become 275 billion times more powerful, which is a lot—but in the next two years alone, it will become 275 billion times more powerful again.

Digital applications gained critical mass only in the last 10 or 15 years, and that's no coincidence; that's when we arrived at the second half of the chessboard. During the dot-com boom and subsequent bust, computing power wasn't strong enough for Apple to produce the iPhone—but by 2007 it was. Only when we began to enter the second half of the chessboard could technology enable powerful mass-market consumer tech applications, which in turn enabled the tremendous wealth creation we've experienced over the last generation.

Now that we're on the second half of the chessboard, even more radical change and innovation seem inevitable. Those skeptical about this assertion should consider the last time civilization experienced it, about a century ago, when the compounding of mechanical power took hold and spawned one industrial innovation after another. Consider the two images opposite, both of New York City's Easter Day Parade. The first, taken in 1900, shows only a single automobile among a sea of horse-drawn carriages. The second, taken in 1913, shows only a single horse among a sea of automobiles.

As we move along the chessboard squares, new industries will be born, and these new industries will generate new waves of disruption. Companies such as Apple, Google, and Facebook, which are now on the attack, will have to defend their economic castles. At some point, their

Easter Day Parade, New York City, 1900.

Easter Day Parade, New York City, 1913.

moats will be breached. It's hard to tell when this will occur, but it's inevitable.

One of the reasons I own the tech companies that I do is that they've all demonstrated an ability to disrupt themselves before a competitor does. Intuit divested Quicken, the product the company started with. Alphabet is the clear leader in many next "big thing" projects, including driverless cars and artificial intelligence. The rapid, inevitable pace of technological change also explains why I own large positions in many non-tech companies that I think are tech-proof. No tech company is going to paint your walls with zeros and ones anytime soon.

Although I'm confident that the companies I own have strong moats for the time being, there's a reason Warren Buffett said that the key to successful investing is to find companies with *durable* competitive advantages rather than *permanent* ones. Permanent competitive advantages don't exist. A decent moat lasts perhaps a generation, an exceptional one lasts several, but none lasts forever. The free market sees to that. The Pony Express was the fastest mail service in the West for a time, but then the telegraph came, and then transcontinental trains, and then air mail. In the 1970s and 1980s, Federal Express revolutionized the industry by allowing people to rush documents when it absolutely, positively had to be there overnight. In the 1990s, however, Adobe invented the PDF, and suddenly overnight became just an expensive form of snail mail.

Good companies embrace such dynamism rather than deny it. Sears was the Amazon of its day, innovating once in the late nineteenth century with its mail-order catalogues and then again in the early twentieth with its network of department stores. Because it was so nimble, Sears's corporate life lasted 130 years. Unable to adapt to e-commerce, however, Sears filed for Chapter 11 protection in 2018.

Amazon is the Sears of our day, moving fast to secure a leadership position in e-commerce. A dozen years after its founding, Amazon then became the market leader in cloud computing, an entirely new industry. Because Amazon has competitive advantages and low market shares in both its markets, the company should continue to prosper for at least another decade. At some point, however, Amazon is going to be swept away by technology's fast-moving tides. No ship is strong enough, and no ship's captain clever enough, to withstand them forever.

One day, investors will speak of Amazon, Alphabet, and the rest in the same dismissive way I spoke in the introduction about Toys "R" Us,

Subaru, and Stop & Shop, Peter Lynch's examples of great businesses a generation ago. These are businesses whose best days are now behind them—but one day the same will be true of Amazon, Alphabet, and the rest.

Jeff Bezos is aware of this. "I predict Amazon will fail," he said at a recent employee meeting. "Amazon will go bankrupt." The only thing employees can do to forestall this moment, Bezos said, was to keep obsessing over customers and putting them first.

———

The world has changed, but it will change again. When it does, Value 3.0 will become obsolete, and we'll need new frameworks to capture the new dynamics. While Value 3.0 is where the money is today, one day it will be elsewhere. Then it will be time for Value 4.0.

Glossary of Terms

This glossary includes many terms to help you understand the basics of accounting, which is the language of business. It also includes abstract concepts having to do with how companies create and protect business value. Much of intelligent investing involves using your judgment, which has nothing to do with debits and credits.

Balance sheet—One of the three key financial statements for any firm (the others are the income statement or **profit and loss** statement and the **statement of cash flows**). The balance sheet is a snapshot of a company's assets and liabilities—what it *owns* and what it *owes*. When you subtract a company's liabilities from its assets, you derive a figure known as net worth, also known as **book value.**

Before World War II, in Ben Graham's day, net worth was a critical metric for **value investing,** because it measured what a company's **tangible assets** could be liquidated for. As the economy has transitioned from hard assets to brands, and now to companies whose main assets are software, the balance sheet has become much less important as a way to value companies.

Book value—An asset-based metric that's calculated by taking what a company owns (its assets) and subtracting what it owes (its liabilities). Value investors have historically compared a company's book value to its stock price to understand how much they're being asked to pay in relation to a company's net assets. See **price to book value.**

Capital cost or expense—An outlay a company makes that accounting rules deem to have a greater than a one-year useful life. Rent and salaries are considered **operating costs** and are expensed when incurred, but capital costs are depreciated or amortized over multiple years. Factories are good examples of a capital cost.

Note, however, that accounting rules haven't kept up with the economic realities of the Digital Age. Tech companies incur R & D and sales expenses that must be written off immediately but that often have a useful life of greater than one year.

Capital markets—The term "Wall Street" is a stand-in for "the capital markets." As the name implies, capital markets exist as a place where companies go find funds—capital—when they need them. Helped by investment banks, corporations come to Wall Street and shop for the best price at which they can raise either **equity** (common stock, which is what most people invest in) or debt (a much larger market, but usually traded only by professionals).

Competitive advantage—Competitive advantage is the key to earning sustained excess profits in a market economy. Given the competitive nature of capitalism, most companies earn only average returns; the excess profits are given away, so to speak, to the consumer, as companies seek to attract, please, and retain them. If a company has a competitive advantage, however, it does not have to share all the economic benefits it enjoys. Instead, it keeps them for its shareholders. Identifying such companies is key to being a successful investor.

Other terms for this phenomenon are "edge" or, thanks to Warren Buffett, "a moat" around the business that keeps competition away. In the Industrial Age, companies gained a competitive advantage from economies of scale: creating efficiencies in manufacturing or distribution such that their per-unit costs of production were lower than their competitors'. As the consumer economy became more important after World War II, a different kind of edge predominated, one based on **in-**

tangible assets like a company's brand. Buffett made dozens of successful investments in such companies.

In the Digital Age, competitive advantage tends to be most evident not in manufacturing economies of scale or even in brand loyalty but in other, newer edges like **network effects**.

Compounding—Compounding refers to the growth of anything—profits, computing power—and specifically how growth from a larger base becomes ever more powerful. If you invest $10 in a stock and it doubles, you've made $10. But if you invest $1 million in that same stock and it doubles, you've made $1 million.

Earnings power—To determine whether they're getting a good deal, most investors look at a business's current earnings or **profits** and compare them to what the stock is trading for. The resulting ratio, known as the price/earnings or **P/E ratio,** is perhaps the most common valuation metric in all of security analysis. This ratio, however, was conceived in an age when most publicly traded businesses were mature and generating high levels of profitability. They didn't need to invest vast sums in sales, marketing, and product development. Most digital businesses, by contrast, are still in their infancy and are therefore spending heavily to build out their markets. This spending is usually wise but, because of antiquated accounting conventions, it penalizes the current income statement and makes the P/E ratio look artificially high.

It's therefore analytically incorrect to compare the P/E ratio of a mature business operating at scale to an immature one that's reinvesting. To put emerging growth companies on an apples-to-apples basis with mature legacy companies, and to gauge their ultimate intrinsic ability to generate wealth, we need to look beyond what such companies report as earnings today to their "earnings power." A mature software company brings nearly 50 cents of every sales dollar to the operating income line, but a rapidly growing company like Intuit reports **profit**

margins only half of that. Earnings power seeks to remedy such distortions.

Earnings yield—A company's **price/earnings ratio** is a common shortcut to see how much the market is asking us to pay for a certain company. It's often worthwhile to flip the equation, from P/E to E/P. A $15 stock currently earning $1 per share has a P/E of fifteen times but a "yield" of $1/$15, or 7%. In a time when the U.S. government is paying you less than 2% to hold long-term Treasury bonds, that yield's attractive.

Note that a company's **profits** are not equivalent to a bond's regular payments. Profits can fluctuate, and the company doesn't always hand you the money in the form of dividends; just as often, a company will retain its profits to invest in the business, purchase another company, or repurchase its own stock. Nevertheless, earnings yield is a helpful theoretical construct because it makes a stock comparable to a bond.

Equity—In finance, "equity" has two meanings. When it comes to securities, an equity is a company's common stock. "Owning equity" means you own a piece of the business. Equity is distinguished from debt in that equity has all the exposure to a business's incremental **profits** but also suffers disproportionately should the business run into trouble. In a bankruptcy, equity investors are often wiped out.

When it comes to corporate financial statements, "equity" also means a company's net worth. This is found on a company's **balance sheet** and is simply a measure of a company's assets, what it *owns*, minus its liabilities, what it *owes*.

First-mover or fast-mover advantage—The phenomenon that describes the edge a company gains when it moves early to capture a new market. The term comes from chess, in which the player playing the white pieces is thought to have an advantage because he or she moves first. Similarly, a business that acts first, or acts with the most urgency, often becomes the market leader.

Flywheel—See **network effects.**

Franchise—In investing, a franchise is a company that's distinguished by superior profitability, a high **return on equity,** and the general certainty of its future profit stream. When department stores ruled, Sears was a franchise investment; when soft drinks were not considered a health hazard, Coca-Cola was a franchise investment. Today, with the digital economy on firm footing and trends like e-commerce and online advertising rampant, Amazon and Google have become franchise investments.

Fundamental analysis—Fundamental analysis focuses on the quality of a business and its place in its industry's ecosystem. Fundamental analysts care about factors that can be expressed numerically—**profit margins, return on equity,** and so on—but as the name suggests, fundamental analysis seeks to identify a company's fundamental strengths. Warren Buffett is the most famous and the most successful fundamental analyst.

Growth investing—A money management approach that places primacy on a company's growth prospects and gives secondary consideration to the **price/earnings ratio** that must be paid for the business.

Growth rate—The rate at which a company increases its sales or **profits.** All else being equal, the higher the growth rate, the more valuable the company. That said, however, a 10% growth rate that lasts for fifty years is more valuable than a 20% growth rate that lasts for only five. Confusing fast-growing companies with durable, valuable **franchises** is a common mistake when investing in stocks.

Intangible assets—In contrast to **tangible assets,** intangibles, as the name suggests, have little to no physical form. A customer's loyalty is an intangible asset: you can't touch it or precisely quantify it, but it's valuable. The same is true with a brand or trademark, like Coca-Cola's red-and-white can or Nike's swoosh.

As the developed world has transitioned from an industrial-based economy to a service-oriented one, intangible assets have become more and more important. The digital revolution has accelerated this trend because software platforms require few physical assets to run. U. S. Steel requires huge factories to produce its goods—even Intel must spend billions of dollars to make a semiconductor fabrication facility—but all Google needs to run its search network are some smart engineers with laptops and central servers to store and process the data. Google's key asset, its search network, is therefore largely intangible.

Leverage—A Wall Street term for debt. Debt is called leverage because it amplifies, or levers, your **equity** returns. If you own a home worth $400,000 and you've paid half in cash, $200,000 is your equity. The other $200,000 you've borrowed is your leverage. If the house appreciates to $500,000, the equity, leveraged by the debt, gets all of the $100,000 incremental returns. If the house depreciates to $300,000, however, the equity likewise absorbs all the losses.

LTV/CAC—An abbreviation for the equation "lifetime value of a customer divided by customer acquisition costs." It is a metric used by many digital businesses to measure how effective their marketing expenditures are. Lifetime value, or LTV, is the revenue the company expects to generate from a customer. Customer acquisition costs, or CAC, is the amount of money a company spends to acquire this customer. Most digital companies aim for a ratio of $3/$1—that is, they want to generate $3 in lifetime revenue for every dollar they spend on marketing.

Margin of safety—A term pioneered by Ben Graham, the father of **value investing,** that calls a money manager's attention not to how much he can make in an investment but to how much he stands to lose. If I buy a house for $100,000 that I know includes $150,000 worth of gold in the attic, I am said to be investing with a margin of safety, because the gold in the attic is worth $50,000 more than I paid for the house.

Market capitalization—Often shortened to "market cap," it is the dollar value of a publicly traded company's stock. Market cap is computed by multiplying a company's stock price by its fully diluted shares outstanding.

Investors use market cap as a proxy for a company's value. The larger the market cap, the more valuable the company. Stock prices, of course, often fluctuate, and stock prices are often wrong. That's how investors make money: by finding discrepancies between a stock's quoted price and its fair value.

Momentum investing—Also known as "the greater fool theory," this school of money management cares neither about **fundamental analysis** nor **quantitative analysis.** Momentum investors care about only one thing: whether a stock is going up or going down. As the term suggests, momentum investors seek to ride such trends. As such, momentum investing is short-term in nature, and momentum investors are generally and rightly regarded as speculators.

Net income—"The bottom line," or what a company reports after deducting all expenses from revenues. These expenses include interest, taxes, and **operating expenses** like salaries and rent. It is also after depreciation, which is a proxy for the **capital costs** a company must incur to maintain its long-term assets, like factories. Because non-operating items like interest and taxes can distort the picture, many analysts use **operating income** as an apples-to-apples proxy for the true profit-generating potential of a business.

Network effects—A term used to describe how a business becomes more valuable as more people use it. A stock exchange is an early example of a business that grew in value as more and more people decided to trade on that exchange. Today, many software companies benefit from network effects. The more guests who visit Airbnb's website, the more incentive there is for property owners to list their rentals on Airbnb. The listing increase draws more guests seeking accommodation, which in turn drives more property owners to list, and so on. For this reason, network effects are also known as "the flywheel" or "a virtuous circle."

Network effects are a key source of **competitive advantage** for many digital companies today. Historically, businesses gained an advantage through economies of scale that were based on the size of their factories or distribution systems. The larger the factories and distribution systems, the lower the per-unit production costs, so the company with the most scale won. The same dynamic applies today, but it's reversed: it's not the production capacity that matters but the number of customers who are attracted to the platform. For this reason, network effects are also called "demand side economies of scale." It's the customer demand, not the size of a company's production capacity, that drives the competitive advantage.

Operating cost or expense—Costs that are deemed to have less than a one-year useful life. Rent, salaries, and the like are operating costs. Longer-term expenditures like those for factories and warehouses are **capital costs,** and the expense for such items is depreciated, or stretched out over multiple years. In today's digital world, however, accounting rules haven't kept up with economic reality. Many R & D expenses clearly have a multiyear useful life, but accounting requires nearly all of them to be expensed in the year they were incurred.

Operating income—Also referred to as earnings before interest and taxes, or EBIT, operating income can be a good gauge of the relative strength or weakness of a business. High margins, measured as operating income divided by total revenues, usually indicate a strong business. Note, however, that the ultimate benchmark is **return on capital,**

which takes into account the **capital costs** required to generate the income.

Platform company—An enterprise that becomes essential to so many consumers that other companies feel compelled to do business on it—for a fee, of course. Apple is a classic example: any company selling an app through the App Store must pay Apple 30% of its sales.

Price/earnings ratio (P/E)—A shorthand, first-cut approach an analyst often uses to assess the cheapness or expensiveness of a stock. Every stock has a price, which is the P in "P/E." The denominator is the current **earnings,** or after-tax profits, of the company in question.

If a stock is trading at $15 and the current earnings is $1, the P/E multiple is $15/$1, or fifteen times earnings. If that's confusing, a useful, commonsensical way to think about a P/E multiple is to invert it so that it becomes like a bond yield. See **earnings yield.**

All else being equal, a higher multiple equals a more expensive stock. Caveat emptor, however: a stock is a fractional ownership of a business whose fortunes wax and wane with the times. In the last ten years, buying stocks with low earnings multiples—historically, a key tool in the **value investing** toolbox—has not worked. Legacy companies like Sears have appeared cheap on a multiple of current earnings, but they have been cheap because their future is bleak. Conversely, stocks like Alphabet and Amazon have appeared expensive throughout their history, but they may deserve a higher multiple because their future is bright. Accounting distortions and heavy investment spending by digital companies further impair the utility of this once-reliable ratio. For more discussion, see **earnings power.**

Price to book value—A common value-investing metric that measures price paid vs. value received in terms of a company's assets. A common yardstick in the Value 1.0 framework, price to book value has fallen out of favor as companies become less dependent on physical assets like factories and inventory to produce profits.

Profit and profit margins—Profit is what's left after a company pays its expenses. It can be expressed either as a function of **net income** or **operating income.** Either way, profit margins are a key ratio: usually, the more a company can keep of every sales dollar, the stronger the business is. An average operating profit margin is in the 10% range; anything below this indicates that a company faces competitive pressure or has products that don't command a premium. Profit margins above 15% indicate the opposite. A mature software company operating at scale can have an operating profit margin of nearly 50%, an indication of the superior economics of digital enterprises. Careful, though—return on capital is the single most telling metric.

Profit and loss statement—Along with the **balance sheet** and the **statement of cash flows,** this statement—commonly referred to as "the P&L"—seeks to capture how much a company makes in a year. This figure is expressed as **net income,** or **profits.**

Quantitative analysis—A quantitative analyst—or, more commonly now, a computer program designed to perform quantitative analysis—focuses solely on numerical inputs in determining when and how to invest. Modern quantitative firms like AQR Capital and Renaissance Technologies use vast computing power to identify and exploit thousands of small, intraday price movements among various asset classes. Quantitative analysis has been practiced in many forms. Ben Graham, the father of modern security analysis and value investing, was essentially a "quant."

Return on capital—Similar to return on equity, **return on capital** seeks to identify whether a business has the characteristics of a **franchise.** Return on equity gives a company credit for using debt, or **leverage,** while return on capital removes debt from the equation.

Return on equity—Another key investing metric that combines the profit and loss **statement** with the **balance sheet.** Return on equity and **return on capital** are ratios that seek to answer the key question: How much will it cost me to generate a dollar of profit? It's one thing to generate **profit,** which you can find on the P&L; it's quite another to make money while using as little capital as possible.

The numerator for return on equity is a company's profit. The denominator is the net capital—its equity—that it uses to generate that profit. Any return on equity, or ROE, below 10% generally indicates that a business either has poor profit margins or requires too much capital to generate its profit. Any ROE above 15% indicates a strong business; an ROE of 20%+ usually indicates a superior business, or **franchise.**

Reversion to the mean—A financial/mathematical concept positing that, over time, things go back to normal. If a retail company that typically grows its sales at 5% a year has a few off years, betting on reversion to the mean means betting that sales growth will return to historical averages. Like low **price/earnings ratios,** reversion to the mean has been a key tool in **value investors'** toolboxes, because for much of the twentieth century the economy was relatively stable. With the rise of the Internet, however, using a mean reversion strategy can be dangerous. Legacy industries like brick-and-mortar retailers and fossil fuel companies show no signs of returning to normal, nor do digital companies. While the former have deteriorating business conditions, the latter are still early in their growth trajectory.

Securities analyst—Someone who spends their time researching publicly traded financial instruments of corporations, usually either stocks or bonds. Analysts come in two general forms. **Fundamental analysts** concern themselves with the *qualitative factors* that drive a company's growth and profitability: the strength of its business, for example, or management quality. **Quantitative analysts,** on the other hand, are mainly interested in "just the numbers," the many statistics thrown off by corporate financial statements and the markets in which the securities trade.

Standard & Poor's 500 (S&P 500)—A compendium of five hundred American stocks, many of them large multinationals, meant to capture in one index the broad variety of publicly traded U.S. companies. The keepers of this index meet every quarter to ensure that it has the right weighting of technology companies, financial companies, and so on to accurately reflect the U.S. stock market and the American economy.

"The S&P" or, even more simply, "the index," is the benchmark that all investors should gauge their money manager by. All investors face an existential question: Can they find a manager who over time beats the index after deducting his or her fees for managing the money, or do they resign themselves to taking the average? If the latter, they simply buy an index fund, which mirrors the S&P 500 and has virtually no fees associated with it.

Worldwide, there are many similar indices. The United Kingdom has the FTSE 100, France has the CAC 40, and there are global indices such as the MSCI World Index. However, if you accept the premise that the United States' stock market has historically been the world's best performing, then the S&P 500 is the index by which everyone should be measured.

Statement of cash flows—The third and final major corporate financial statement, the cash flow statement shows how much money entered and exited the company's treasury over a given period. In this way, it is more precise than the **profit and loss statement,** which uses various non-cash estimates and accruals.

Tangible assets—As the term suggests, a tangible asset is anything whose cash value is fairly easy to estimate and can thus be liquidated, or sold. Buildings, factories, and inventory are all tangible assets; so are cash and receivables, which are what a company is owed by its customers. Although cash and receivables aren't strictly physical, their asset value is known; contrast this with **intangible assets,** which, though valuable, are much harder to quantify.

Value investing—One of the oldest and most successful forms of investing. Although it's hard to define precisely, value investing is characterized by rigor, discipline, patience, and an insistence that an investor pay a cheap or at least a fair price for the business in question. It uses both quantitative metrics and more qualitative metrics to varying degrees, depending on which subset of value investing is being practiced.

Value investing began a century ago when Ben Graham began to systematically analyze the **balance sheets** of American corporations. He passed his techniques down to his star pupil, Warren Buffett, who has in turn passed them down to subsequent generations. Over the years, however, the definition of what constitutes a cheap or fair price has changed considerably. Graham thought it had to do mainly with a company's liquidation value; Buffett historically has favored **franchise** companies that were reasonably priced on a current P/E basis; today, with software platforms dominating the globe in ways neither Graham nor Buffett could have foreseen, value investing is again going through a period of transition and re-examination.

Winner take all—Like the **network effects** and the **platform** phenomenon, winner take all dynamics are closely identified with digital companies. Because consumers tend to gravitate toward one service per digital application—Facebook for social media, Google for search—these companies can amass huge market shares in their respective niches. Thus "winner take all" or "winner take most."

Acknowledgments

Although it's somewhat antiseptic, it feels appropriate to thank all those who helped me by category. All good investors think taxonomically, and this is a book about investing, after all.

Don't, however, mistake the categorizations as a sign that I lack heartfelt gratitude. I am deeply obliged and grateful to all those who helped.

Friends and family

First and deepest thanks go to my wife, Sadie Bridger, and our son, Isaac Bridger Seessel. They were there at the book's conception and saw it through to term with patience and loving care. I'll never forget reading horrible early drafts to them aloud in our backyard and having them tell me how great the book was, or could be.

To Doug Hirsch, who got me into this business more than twenty-five years ago and who has encouraged and counseled me wisely ever since. Doug knew me when I was a poor journalist and then a struggling freelance writer selling Cutco knives on the side.

To Seth Stephens-Davidowitz, a talented writer who read early versions of the manuscript and gave me good, positive feedback at a time when I needed it.

To my buddy George Klas, who never stopped cheering me on, even when I was too busy to show up for our walks in Central Park.

And to John Canning, whom I've known since I was ten, who

read various drafts and who provided the Latin translation of "faster, cheaper, better."

Professional contacts

Note: I count most of the people below as friends, but I list them here since I know them principally through work.

First, to my old bosses: Chuck Cahn and John Mahedy at Sanford Bernstein, Ron Baron at Baron Funds, and Chris Davis at Davis Selected Advisers. All of them helped me grow from a green former newspaper reporter into something resembling a sophisticated analyst.

To Tom Gayner, co-CEO and chief investment officer of Markel Corporation, who has been a source, a sounding board, and a mentor in my transition to Value 3.0.

To Chris Begg of East Coast Asset Management, who shared with me his own journey to Value 3.0 and, indeed, gifted me the nomenclature of Value 1.0, Value 2.0, and Value 3.0 itself.

To Sourav Choudhary, a partner at TCI Fund Management, who more than anyone influenced my ideas on what constitutes a superior business in today's economy and how to value it.

To Jim Keenan, Clint Leman, and Gary Sieber, my Indiana friends, who read early chapter drafts and provided constructive criticism as the book took shape.

To Mark Disston, who put considerable time and effort into helping me outline the book when it was still in proposal form. Mark was not shy, and was dead-on when it came to pressing me about how to articulate the most pressing issues facing investors today.

To Tim Stone, a long-term Amazonian whom I met in the dot-com bust, when the company had a market cap of only $4 billion. Tim subsequently went on to become the CFO of Ford Motor and has a unique perspective on the old and the new economies, which he was generous in sharing with me.

To John Smith, my go-to cryptocurrency expert, who asked that I use a pseudonym to protect him from crypto pirates who might want to plunder his Bitcoin, Ethereum, and other pieces of eight. The fact that John, a reasonable person, felt compelled to ask me this says a lot about cryptocurrency and its maturity, or lack thereof, as an asset class.

To two of my former analysts, Manuel Navas and Meraz Mamun, who read various parts of the manuscript and who gave me valuable insights from their respective circles of competence.

To Baruch Lev, an NYU accounting professor, who shared with me both his research papers and his general thoughts about why his discipline, which is essential for keeping score in business, requires a major overhaul.

To Henryk Jankowski, aka Fromchmm, a talented accountant and auditor who helped me think through various accounting issues and how they applied to the Digital Age.

To Craig Lazzara at S&P Dow Jones Indices, who has done good work on Warren Buffett's long-term record and shared it with me.

To David Kanter, founder and principal of consulting firm Real World Insights, who was generous and patient with me as I sought to understand the finer points of Moore's and Metcalfe's laws and their implications for the future of tech.

The editorial process

To my agent, Jennifer Joel at ICM, who like my wife and son was present at the creation of *Where the Money Is*. Jenn was instrumental in shaping the proposal; she helped me edit various versions of the book; and she understood when I needed advice, when I needed encouragement, and when I needed a kick in the pants. The book is materially better for her involvement.

To my editor, Ben Loehnen at Avid Reader Press, and his assistant, Carolyn Kelly. They shepherded the book through its several drafts with care, tact, and skill. Somehow, Ben always knew when it was time to intervene with editorial suggestions and when to let me figure it out myself. As anyone who's ever worked under an editor knows, that is a rare skill and one that's highly prized by writers, including me.

ACKNOWLEDGMENTS

To Erik Brynildsen, who brought the book to life with his graphics and in the process proved that a picture is indeed worth 1,000 words, and to Jeff Spector at FactSet, who produced the data that Erik used.

To Dan Lam, a fact-checker I've known for years who has as sharp a pencil as I've ever seen.

To Brian Guzman, my longtime lawyer at Guzman Advisory Partners, who counseled me on important legal and commercial matters and who more generally cheered me along the way.

To Gabe Alpert and Nikka Rosenstein, who read early versions of the book and gave me good advice about what I should say to younger investors and how to say it.

To the people at *Barron's*: Almar Latour, Jack Otter, Lauren Rublin, and Andrew Bary. Jack in particular restarted my journalism career five years ago and encouraged me to keep going.

To Alan Murray and Matt Heimer at *Fortune*, who published a long article of mine in 2018 entitled "An Evolve-or-Die Moment for the World's Great Investors," which turned out to be the seed for this book.

Index

NOTE: Page references in *italics* refer to figures and tables.

About the Author

Adam Seessel is a graduate of Dartmouth College and began his professional life as a newspaper reporter in North Carolina. There, he won the George Polk Award for environmental reporting. In 1995, Seessel took his research skills to Wall Street, where he worked for Sanford C. Bernstein, Baron Capital, and Davis Selected Advisers before starting his own firm, Gravity Capital Management, which manages money for high–net worth individuals and institutions. Since beginning a record of stock-market performance while at Davis Funds in mid-2000, he has beaten the S&P 500. He has also written about investing as a contributor to *Barron's* and *Fortune*. Married and with one grown son who works as a software engineer, Seessel and his wife, an artist, live in Manhattan.